# TOWARD A LATINA FEMINISM
## OF THE AMERICAS

CHICANA MATTERS SERIES

DEENA J. GONZÁLEZ AND ANTONIA CASTAÑEDA,
EDITORS

Chicana Matters Series focuses on one of the largest population groups in the United States today, documenting the lives,
values, philosophies, and artistry of contemporary Chicanas.
Books in this series may be richly diverse, reflecting the experiences of Chicanas themselves, and incorporating a broad spec-
trum of topics and fields of inquiry. Cumulatively, the books
represent the leading knowledge and scholarship in a significant and growing field of research and, along with the literary
works, art, and activism of Chicanas, underscore their significance in the history and culture of the United States.

# TOWARD A LATINA FEMINISM OF THE AMERICAS

*Repression and Resistance in Chicana and Mexicana Literature*

ANNA MARIE SANDOVAL

UNIVERSITY OF TEXAS PRESS

*Austin*

Requests for permission to reproduce material from this
work should be sent to:
    Permissions
    University of Texas Press
    P.O. Box 7819
    Austin, TX 78713-7819
    www.utexas.edu/utpress/about/bpermission.html

♾ The paper used in this book meets the minimum re-
quirements of ANSI/NISO Z39.48-1992 (R1997)
(Permanence of Paper).

Sandoval, Anna Marie.
    Toward a Latina feminism of the Americas : repression
and resistance in Chicana and Mexicana literature / Anna
Marie Sandoval. — 1st ed.
        p.   cm. — (Chicana matters series)
    Includes bibliographical references and index.
    ISBN 978-0-292-71884-5 (cloth : alk. paper)
        1. American literature—Mexican American authors—
History and criticism.   2. American literature—Women
authors—History and criticism.   3. Mexican literature—
Women authors—History and criticism.   4. Feminism
in literature.   5. Women in literature.   6. Literature,
Comparative—American and Mexican.   7. Literature,
Comparative—Mexican and American.   I. Title.
    PS153.M4S36   2008
    810.9'8972—dc22
                                            2008018453

*For my mother, Evila Sandoval,*
*and in loving memory of my father,*
*Cipriano Sandoval.*

# CONTENTS

# PREFACE

*I myself invent time by first conjuring up the*
*voices and spirits of the women living under*
*brutal repressive regimes . . . [b]ecause I want to*
*do justice to their voices. To tell these women,*
*in my own gentle way, that I will fight for them,*
*that they provide me with my own source of*
*humanity.*

HELENA MARÍA VIRAMONTES

I, like Helena María Viramontes, wish to give voice to the
women who, for whatever reasons, cannot tell their stories.
I realize that it is a privilege (although it should be a right) in
what I define as my communities to have access to language
and the written word. This realization carries with it many
responsibilities and many gifts. So it is not only for myself
that I have committed to do cultural work as a scholar and
educator.

While working on this project, I have often thought of my
sister Rebecca as my audience. She is not formally trained in
literature nor is she an academic. She is, however, a woman
who shares many similarities with the important women I
write about.

I also wish to make historically marginalized theory accessible to undergraduates, including my own students. I see this
work as belonging to those whom I define as my community
and as a welcome to those who have a desire to engage in a
dialogue about Chicana and Mexicana literature.[1]

The challenge of connecting the community and the academy is constant and has been taken on by many of us women of color. We are constantly straddling borders, moving between the elitism of the academy and the familiarity of the communities where we were raised. My own narrative speaks of this space—a space where my passion for my subject has been fueled, and where heartache and hope coexist.

My passion comes not just from a respect for and scholarly interest in the field of Chicana studies, but from my lived experience as a Chicana. Discussing literary themes of rape, incest, domestic violence, colonization, orphanhood, sexuality, and poverty of women and children is always painful, because literature mirrors society; sometimes it is the conscience of society. Never have I wondered whether these are important issues to discuss. But when self-doubt set in during the research for this book, I questioned whether my voice could in any way make a difference in the recognition of these issues.

Because the literature by Chicanas and Mexicanas is a transformational literature for me, this work has been more than just an academic exercise. Although I read some Chicano texts on my own as a teenager, it was not until my undergraduate years that I was formally introduced to this body of literature. The first Chicano studies course I took at the University of California, Santa Barbara (UCSB), in 1985, was "Chicano Theater," with Dr. Yolanda Broyles-González. I was a junior and, not surprisingly, this was the first course to validate my experience as a Chicana from a working-class background. After that course, I enrolled in Chicano studies courses every quarter. I was fortunate to have had the support of two professors in the English Department and strong encouragement from the then-few Chicano studies faculty and staff at the university to continue my scholarly pursuits in a graduate program in literature.[1]

My experience at UCSB helped prepare me in many different ways for my graduate career at the University of California, Santa Cruz—including the biases I would encounter, especially the questioning of my specialization as a legitimate area of study. I was relieved to learn on the day of my graduate program orientation that, in my class of twelve entering women, five were women of color also invested in honoring and bringing to the forefront formerly silenced voices. I was fortunate to have as part of my cohort Gloria Anzaldúa, who was a source of inspiration for me and for other women in the program. Already an accomplished scholar and writer, her contributions in class were significant. As a woman who had experienced her own struggles in the academic realm, she also taught me strategies for survival and had an early influence on my thinking. Her telling of her "autohistoria" gave me both the courage to tell my story and the form in which to tell it.

Study abroad in Mexico came during my second year in graduate school—perfect timing for me. After my first year, I needed time away from the privileged environment, and, for me, Mexico was a refuge. Certainly, there were challenges— learning a "new" language in which I had to take classes, write, and present papers—but for the first time, I was no longer visibly the "other." That in itself was validating. Taking courses in Mexican literature, particularly a course that focused on women, inspired me to pursue this rich literature further. Reading about the Mexicana experience at the same time that I was building alliances and developing relationships with Mexicanas made me realize the connections that needed to be discussed systematically. There began the idea for this project.

After fourteen months in Mexico, coming back to Santa Cruz was a difficult and painful process. I had to remind myself repeatedly that I had as much right as anyone to be pursuing a doctorate, even though I frequently felt that others were trying to tell me that I did not belong. After successfully completing my qualifying exams, I was awarded the Chicana dissertation fellowship at UCSB and returned to that campus for one year.

I was immersed in an active Chicana/o scholarly community and working with cutting-edge scholars such as Yolanda Broyles-González, Antonia Castañeda, Deena González, and Carl Gutiérrez-Jones. I also had the opportunity to teach in my area. I met students who were hungry for Chicana literature; these young Chicanas reminded me of myself as an English major trying desperately to find something in the course listings to which I could relate.

The following year, I returned to my home campus in Santa Cruz for two additional years to complete the dissertation and to support myself by teaching. The project was postponed when, in a brief span of time, my sister discovered she had breast cancer and my parents divorced after forty-eight years of marriage. These situations would inform my work in ways I could not have imagined at the time. Throughout the writing process, I was given strength and voice through the women in my life: girls and women in my family, *compañeras, colegas*. Women's support communities were developing in ways that I had never experienced within my family. Although talking about women's repression and resistance on a national or global level can be painful, such discussions at home bring a different set of challenges.

When my sister Rebecca's cancer was diagnosed and she was told she would have to go through radiation treatments, I moved from the San Francisco Bay area to live with her and her daughter in Sacramento. At about the same time, my parents separated, and my mom also moved in with my sister. My sister's battle with cancer brought us closer and gave us a greater appreciation of life and our relationship. My mother moved in before I did to help my sister, immediately after her lumpectomy. There we were, three women and an adolescent (my niece) who made up three generations facing a deadly disease and a divorce that would at times divide the family. I wanted to give all of my attention to my sister, and she wanted to give all of her attention to her health, but everything seemed to merge. Everyone was suffering together or apart, and nobody was healing very quickly. I would hold my sister some nights while she cried or we would cry together. Her daughter would ask me questions like, "What would you do if your mother died?" I was just as much there for my niece as I was for my sister. And for my mother.

My trips home before then had generally been pleasant. I went home as often as possible for birthdays and other holidays and celebrations. Usually, everyone, including me, was on their best behavior. My family and I would often sit around the table laughing (uncontrollably at times) and enjoying catching up on each other's lives. I was the only one living away from Sacramento, so I should have been the only one having to catch up, but with lives so busy with school, sports, and work, everyone always had news. Also, they did not see each other as often as one would imagine.

Going home this time to help Rebecca was not just a visit, although it would turn out to be only three months (longer for me, however, than some of my previous "permanent" residences). It was a time to become caretaker to my sister, disciplinarian to my niece, and more friend than daughter to my mother. The daily routine included: taking my sister to work in the morning, picking her up at noon to drive her to her radiation treatment, taking her to lunch and returning her to work to complete her eight hour work day. Our family had faced many obstacles in the past, among them a brother who died at age sixteen, a sickly father, and medical challenges of multiple family members. Rebecca once said, after some family tragedy I no longer recall, that our family's theme song was "If it ain't one thing, it's another." We tried to laugh the pain away sometimes, but usually we just denied that our family was any different from other families.

Because I am the youngest of the six living children in my family, living away from home had provided me a different perspective. Although I had felt a need my whole life to mend things, I had given that up when I realized my parents had made a decision to live together in an unhappy and unhealthy relationship. Thus their decision to divorce, though unexpected, was not a complete surprise for me.

The news of my sister's cancer, however, rocked my foundation. My big sister, whom I had relied on and learned from, needed my unwavering support. Thankfully, the disease was caught early. Unfortunately for many women, especially women of color and poor women, this is not the case. Her initial reaction and mine was fear of death. But after some time, she began reading what she could on the subject of breast cancer and healing.

I had always been impressed with Rebecca—with all of her professional and personal accomplishments—and with her biggest challenge facing her, she remained levelheaded and positive. She impressed me as she had never before. With my parents' marriage officially deteriorating, much attention, both positive and negative, was given to them, mostly to my sickly father. Because my mother appeared physically healthy and because, to protect her children, she never said much, some assumed that her emotional and spiritual pain was not as serious as my father's physical condition. Because of the attention paid to my parents, Rebecca's condition did not take top priority with everyone.

When the treatments were over and Rebecca was recovering, I decided it was time to return to the dissertation. My father would tell me from time to time, "I just hope I live to see you graduate." I assumed from this statement that he would be ready to die once I finished. This was not an incentive but, indeed, a reason to prolong the process. I realized that my staying in Sacramento would not mend anything. The only way I would complete the degree would be if I physically left the place of all the conflict—home.

My *prima* (cousin) in New Mexico offered her home for an indefinite period of time so that I could complete the dissertation. There I was more productive than I had been in many other places. Many offered their homes, offices, computers, and, most important, their moral support during this difficult time.

Something else I gained while in New Mexico, perhaps the most important thing, was a women's support network. Although at Rebecca's home I had support from women, the conflict was too great to allow much positive exchange. In New Mexico, my community became a group of women with shared politics, scholarly interests, and cultural background. My *prima*'s home was open to other "drifting" and traveling women. Friends and friends of friends were always welcomed. So, during the final days of writing the dissertation, I benefited from the support of many beautiful souls.

Included in my support network were the undergraduates with whom I shared a computer lab during the final stages of writing: Chicana and Chicano students struggling to complete three-page essays. They made me realize on a daily basis that I had come a long way. "What is a dissertation?" they would ask. "How many pages is it?" "How long have you been working on it?" "What's it about?"

During that time I met a young Chicana at the computer lab struggling to complete a paper that was due the following day. She was a junior and an English major and did not know how to cite references. I was angry that her instructors had let her "slide" without learning the correct way to cite, and she was frustrated with herself for not knowing. I heard her telling another student that she had almost dropped out of school the week before because the pressure was too much for her. Not knowing if she would accept my advice, I attempted to give it anyway. I shared my own story of my undergraduate years and how I had experienced similar frustrations. She asked me what I did after earning the Bachelor of Arts degree, and it felt good to tell her that I was only one month away from completing my PhD. I felt like our brief encounter benefited us both. I was motivated to spend a few more hours at the computer, and she was motivated to finish her paper.

Similar exchanges I had at that time with undergraduates were part of what motivated me to complete the dissertation. Today, more than ten years later, it is my students who often motivate me to continue giving voice to the marginalized through my writing. It is not only for me that I pursued the PhD. I cannot separate myself from my community—my community of women and of Raza. Although the writing process is an alienating one—the thesis/article/book becomes the main relationship in one's life—the life process that feeds that relationship and writing process has been seasoned by many family members, friends, and acquaintances who have inspired me in different ways. I remember oftentimes feeling jealous of my colleagues in graduate school who seemed to be working on their degrees strictly for themselves. How incredible, I thought, to feel responsible only for yourself, to not think about the politics of your work, to not worry about being stared at as the "representative" of your community, to not think that when you earned a job everyone would think you got it because you were a woman of color and not because you were qualified. And I thought how nice it must be when people don't express surprise at your knowledge of canonical works or your command of the English language. Although I may sometimes still be jealous of these "luxuries," I also realize that the strength I have gained from political commitment and community connection outweighs any burden I may feel. The frustration, the challenge, is there only when the words do not come as naturally as the passion for my topic.

My conjuring up the voices and spirits of the women living under brutal and repressive regimes has, as Helena María Viramontes did, provided me with a source of humanity, particularly during times of personal and professional challenges. The voices of women in my book have supported me in my own acts of daily resistance. This work is deeply personal. There is a strong connection between my story and the story of the authors and literary characters I write about in the following pages. The personal has intellectual and theoretical linkages that are in fact an essential, constitutive part of the theory and resistance that is woven throughout this work.

# ACKNOWLEDGMENTS

I can only begin to suggest the many people in my circle who have helped me in bringing this project to its completion. With apologies to those who are not named here, I wish to offer my most sincere thanks to the Literature Board of The University of California, Santa Cruz; the University of California Education Abroad Program; the Fulbright Association; the Department of Chicano and Latino Studies at California State University, Long Beach, the College of Liberal Arts at CSULB for their constant institutional support. To Jose Saldívar, Norma Klahn, Louis Owens, Deena Gonzalez, Arturo Aldama, and the anonymous readers of the early manuscript for their guidance. To readers of sections of the manuscript: Barbara Ige, Eve Ashi Griselda Suarez, Maythee Rojas, Tammy Ho, Linda España-Maram, Carolyn Sandoval, Alicia Jimenez, and Rowena Robles for intellectual energy.

To my friends, family, and my students for nurturing my spirit. Finally, to Bernie Visser for love, patience, peace and laughter, I offer my strongest gratitude.

TOWARD A LATINA FEMINISM
OF THE AMERICAS

My interest in comparing Mexicana literature and Chicana literature began during a year of study at la Universidad Nacional Autónoma de México (UNAM) in Mexico City in 1990.[1] As a Chicana from a working-class background, my attraction to living and studying Mexicana literature in Mexico was based not only on my respect for and scholarly interest in the work, but also on my lived experience as a Chicana. Although I did not spend summers and vacations with family in Mexico, as did many of my friends (my roots are in Colorado and New Mexico), like others who self-identify as Chicana/o, I understood my historical and cultural connection to the land that my ancestors knew as México. The experience of living in a place where I was not visibly the other would turn out to be one of the most empowering experiences of my life.

My initial intention was to review the scholarship on Chicanos written by Mexican scholars, but as a student in *filosofía y letras* (arts and sciences), I was enrolled exclusively in literature courses. During one such course on *literatura femenina* (women's literature) I began my exploration of Mexicana literature. Reading about the Mexicana experience then building alliances and developing relationships with Mexicanas made me realize the connections that finally needed to be discussed systematically. Because my emphasis in U.S. literature is on Chicana writers, a comparative literary study of Mexicanas and Chicanas seemed natural and, to be sure, necessary—as not much work had been published in this area.[2]

A comparative analysis of Mexicana and Chicana subjectivities, this book examines oppositional discourses that these writers present in their work. By reformulating cultural symbols and offering nontraditional constructions of culturally relevant themes, Chicanas and Mexicanas are responding to systems of patriarchy. Sharing a cultural history, Chicanas and Mexicanas critique similar issues. Interesting differences in their literature, however, because of their unique subject positions in their respective communities, their different experiences with U.S. colonization, and other unique aspects of their lives, also lead to enhanced understanding of their voices.[3]

To begin my study of Mexicana and Chicana writers, I examine new currents in scholarship and in the theoretical approaches to several related areas. The increased interest in critical literary studies in Chicana/o literature both by Chicanas/os and non-Chicanas/os reflects Chicanas' increased literary production. Much of the work of the past twenty-five years has been invigorating; it has also been "women's work." Men, of course, are still publishing, but their literature does not seem to be experiencing the same popularity as women's literature.

Naturally, anyone today who is teaching courses on Chicana/o literature has a much larger variety of texts from which to select than they did twenty-five years ago. No longer is it necessary to read *only* Rudolfo Anaya, José Antonio Villarreal, Rodolpho González, Ernesto Galarza, and other male authors once seen as the first authors of Chicana/o literature. Furthermore, with the recovery projects of some Chicana critics like Clara Lomas, Rosaura Sánchez, and María Herrera-Sobek, the point of departure for the contemporary study of Chicano literature has become the women's voices of the early nineteenth century southwestern United States.[4] This scholarship has, since its inception, continued to change the field. Along with those of Chicanas in various disciplines who are giving sorely needed attention to issues of race, class, gender, and sexuality, the voices of Chicana literature will seed the field of Chicana/o studies as well as other disciplines such as U.S. history and American studies.

In the field of literary criticism, Norma Alarcón's several essays make important contributions. "Chicana Feminism" (1990) gives attention to the issue of Chicana subjectivity. Literary critic Rosaura Sánchez applies a postmodern reading to Chicana/o literature, yet does not include women in the debate in "Postmodernism and Chicano Literature" (1987). Anthropologist Renato Rosaldo enters the literary discussion through a study of the "warrior hero" in *Culture and Truth* (1989). Sonia Saldívar-Hull begins to articulate a theory of international feminism in "Feminism on the Border" (1991). Angie Chabram, in "I Throw Punches for My Race" (1992), critiques the way in which women were given a subordinate role in the Chicano Movement and examines how some Chicanas are rewriting Chicano nationalism. Carl Gutiérrez-Jones examines Chicana and Chicano literature through the lens of critical legal studies in *Rethinking Borderlands* (1995). Ramón Saldívar's *Chicano Narrative* (1990) places the theoretical debates surrounding the field into a chronological context, beginning with the folk-based narrative, the *corrido,* and continuing into contemporary Chicana narrative. Using a poststructuralist approach, Saldívar develops a model for reading Chicano literature, a model that he calls a "dialectics of difference."[5]

As we can see, the theoretical debates that these critics cover are wide ranging and cross several disciplinary boundaries. The present work enters the debate by offering a comparative model for reading Chicana and Mexicana literature that describes how these two literatures inform each other.[6]

This work belongs to a new area of studies that is opening up the discussion among many Americas, an inclusive area that, ideally, will address issues relevant to North, Central, and South America.[7] A mere handful of critical works were published between 1986 and 1992 on comparative literatures of the Americas. One of the first texts to attempt this type of analysis is *Reinventing the Americas* (1986), edited by Bell Chevigny and Gari Laguardia. This text is key to my work, as it initializes the larger dialogue from which my study stems.

Addressing questions about the canon of American literature, Chevigny and Laguardia discuss the need for its redefinition. They do not, however, specifically address Chicana/o literature.

Other provocative discussions place comparative American studies in the foreground. Among these are Lois Parkinson Zamora's *Writing the Apocalypse* (1989); Gustavo Pérez Firmat's *Do the Americas Have a Common Literature?* (1990); and José Saldívar's *The Dialectics of Our America* (1991).

Pérez Firmat's work examines the "contact and perhaps the clash between some of the cultures of the Americas" (*Do the Americas Have a Common Literature?,* 1). He begins his discussion by pointing to the novelty of such a study, reminding us that literary comparison most often refers to studies that run east to west. In the introduction to *Do the Americas Have a Common Literature?* he states: "[S]cholars of North American literature, while they have been much concerned with the 'Americanness' of their domain, have usually neglected to consider this notion in anything other than the narrow nationalistic and anglophone sense, where America becomes a synonym for the United States. On the other hand, students of Latin American literature have for the most part not looked northward in search of significant contexts for their texts" (2–3). The essays aim to "couple the literatures and cultures of this hemisphere—particularly their North American and Latin American sectors—in order to find regions of agreement or communality" (1–2). Pérez Firmat states that he chooses to work toward strengthening commonality instead of crystallizing difference.

He realizes that many scholars may find problems in the intention of his work and in the book's title. Certainly, many would answer the title and question with an emphatic "No!" Roberto Fernández Retamar argues, for example, that some believe the "histories of the United States and the rest of the hemisphere are so unlike that the corresponding literatures are therefore incommensurable" (Pérez Firmat, *Do the Americas Have a Common Literature?,* 5). Pérez Firmat, while agreeing that the historical and political position between Spanish America and the United States is huge, makes the point that "historical position is not always identical with cultural position" (5).

José Saldívar's *The Dialectics of Our America* not only presents a critical framework for discussing U.S. and Latin American fiction and culture and the canon of American literature but also "questions the notion of America itself" (xii). He states in the preface: "*The Dialectics of Our America* thus charts an array of oppositional critical and creative processes that aim to articulate a new, transgeographical conception of American culture—one more responsive to the hemisphere's geographical ties and political crosscurrents than to narrow national ideologies" (xi). Referring to José Martí's "nuestra América," Saldívar critically examines "Martí's conviction of a profound gap between our America and the other America, which is not ours" (7). The present project adds to this body of literature by examining the historiographic debates of previous decades and by focusing on women's writing and feminist critique.

Closer to my specific area of study is *Talking Back* (1992), by Debra Castillo. Castillo's project is not intended to create "an overarching theory" of Latin American feminism,[8] but rather to explore critical issues and strategies of a "Hispanic" feminist literary practice (2): "Latin American feminisms are developing in multiple directions not always compatible with directions taken by Anglo-European feminisms and frequently in discord with one another" (xxii).[9] Castillo's study includes Mexicanas, Chicanas, and other Latin American women and is essential for the study of comparative American literature. Pérez Firmat mentions the lack of inter-American comparative studies. There has been an absence of the critical study of Latin American women; Castillo's study attempts to fill this gap.

Although many of these texts provide useful approaches in the area of "hemispheric comparative inquiry,"[10] the texts most helpful for comparing literature by Chicanas and Mexicanas have been the anthologies produced from the conference sponsored by El Colegio de México, El Colegio de la Frontera Norte, the University of California, San Diego, and San Diego State University in 1988 and 1990, *Mujer y literatura Mexi-*

*cana y Chicana: culturas en contacto.* Prior to these anthologies, no academic journal had compiled these critics' work.
The first of these invaluable anthologies carries the epigraph:
"Con el deseo de unir los lazos entre las mujeres chicanas y
Mexicanas." The organizers of the conference understood the
role that literature plays in producing cultural exchange: it is
a means through which people, sometimes from very distinct
worlds, can communicate. The worlds of Chicanas and Mexicanas are distinct, yet their strong cultural ties make the exchange of ideas, experience, and information imperative. The
anthologies offer a starting point for readers of literature who
are interested in the relationships between Chicanas and Mexicanas. The editors state their goal in the introduction: "para
experimentar el intercambio intenso de la Mexicana de este
lado y la chicana de aquel. . . . lo que esperamos sea una apor-
tación al conocimiento de las culturas que la nutren; los tópicos
que maneja, los silencios que hacen presente aquello que no se
menciona; el tipo de lenguaje utilizado, la palabra escrita que
nos habla del trabajo de las mujeres que tradicionalmente son
hacedoras silenciosos de la cultura" [in order to experience the
intense exchange between Mexican women on this side and
Chicana women on the other side. . . . which we hope will
lead to an enhanced understanding of the cultures that nourish
them, the themes that they explore, the silences that make ex-
plicit those things that are not mentioned, the kind of language
used, the written word that speaks of the work of women who,
traditionally, have been the silent makers of culture] (12). The
anthology's essays provide analyses of various works, yet no
in-depth comparative study of the two national literatures is
included in either edition.[11] Nonetheless, the work initiates an
important dialogue between Mexicanas and Chicanas because
it offers them and their respective communities a better understanding of their mutual historical and cultural experience.

Beyond the issue of "cultural contact" between Mexicanas
and Chicanas through literature, no one theme is central in
the anthologies; the content is wide-ranging because the conference addressed new areas of study. By examining specific
literary texts, contributors address identity issues, feminist

discourse, colonialism, difference, sexuality, and marginality, issues relevant to all national literatures. However, the narratives that are being viewed through these many discourses articulate a particular Mexicana and Chicana experience.

The second volume of *Mujer y literature mexicana y chicana* (1990), while recognizing the text as only a starting point for further investigation, stresses the importance of viewing Mexicana and Chicana literature in a shared context. In the introduction, Aralia López González states: "[Y]a es posible plantear algunos resultados que aún siendo generales y tentativos, permiten perfilar ciertos rasgos afines y también diferenciar entre producciones literarias que teniendo raíces comunes, se han conformado en procesos históricos diferentes" [It is now possible to suggest some results that, although general and tentative, allow us to outline certain common features, and also to differentiate among literary outputs that, although springing from similar roots, are part of different historical processes] (11).

With this in mind, my study continues this exchange through a comparative look at the multiple contexts of cultural, historical, and geographical borders for Mexicanas and Chicanas. Both redefine nationalism in their respective cultures: Chicanas are looking at the roots of the Chicano Movement and demonstrating how it has been rooted in sexism; Mexicanas are examining and challenging their patriarchal culture. I propose a comparative framework for looking at recent developments in Chicana and Mexicana literature.

Similar to Chicana writers, Mexicana writers have had their own literary boom. Jean Franco, in *Plotting Women* (1989), discusses the development in her critical study of Mexicana literature. A great deal of Mexican women's literature includes a repudiation of nation and family: national myths, for example, are parodied, and writers such as Poniatowska, Boullosa, and Mastretta find creative ways to undermine the patriarchy (183).

Also prevalent in recent texts produced by Mexican women are themes of adolescence, sexuality, domestic violence, and, through these, a call for the creation of women-centered communities.[12] Poniatowska also gives the reader female revolutionaries and rebels—such as Jesusa in the testimonial novel *Hasta no verte Jesús mío* (1969). Mexicana literature, then, is representing a historical reality, breaking the patriarchal stranglehold of the Mexican male literature that portrays women as weak and powerless.

The following is an overview of the common thematics of Mexicana and Chicana writers, an examination of how their discursive positions differ, and how they articulate their political and theoretical positions by challenging dominant ideologies.

## COMPARING FEMINISMS

My starting point is an examination of the subject position of each group. I argue that, while Mexicanas have the privilege of writing within a national discourse that at least includes them, Chicanas write against a national discourse that does not recognize them. The Chicana national identity is often challenged by the United States. Mexicanas, while clearly included in their nation, albeit many times as second-class citizens, are similarly talking back to the patriarchal systems in Mexico.[13] Despite the unique circumstances of each group, common experiences with cultural institutions in a patriarchal society lead them, both formally and thematically, to a common literary expression.

Talking back to dominant ideologies is in itself a highly subversive act and is a common thread in Chicana and Mexicana literature. One result of talking back is the redefinition of family or cultural symbols. Chicanas have different ways of expressing this strategy. "Making *familia* from scratch" is how Cherríe Moraga terms it in *Giving Up the Ghost* (58); "border feminism" is how Sonia Saldívar-Hull and others express the particularities of the development of women-centered spaces in Chicana literature.

Though Mexicanas' and Chicanas' positions differ in their respective nations, their narratives take on similar experimental forms as well as a similar thematics. The shared experience of the influence of the Catholic Church, for example, accounts for many common thematic responses in their literature. Refuting the Catholic Church is viewed as highly subversive in both cultures, as are references to other shared themes such as sexuality, domestic violence, and incest. I argue that within the narratives of Mexicanas and Chicanas are embedded their political and theoretical agendas, which challenge dominant ideologies.[14]

Another central issue that the present comparison addresses is how Chicanas and Mexicanas articulate their political and theoretical positions through representations of various figures of resistance, often re-visionings of traditional cultural symbols. Chicana writers, in their literature, often appear more critical than Mexicanas of traditional cultural symbols such as La Llorona, La Virgen de Guadalupe, and La Malinche.

Chicana and Mexicana feminisms have developed from very different circumstances and have gone in very different directions in their respective countries. Mexico has a long history of struggle for women's liberation. Beginning with the seventeenth-century Mexican nun, scholar, and poet Sor Juana Inés de la Cruz, who chose the convent in order to follow her intellectual pursuits, to the women who fought for women's suffrage, to the organizers of the first women's congress in Yucatán, to Rosario Castellanos, the writer and ambassador of modern Mexico, Mexico has seen, in its long history as a nation, many leaders, intellectuals, stateswomen, writers, and other women who have been intimately involved in all areas of the country's development.[15] Despite this, surprisingly little has been written on the history of feminist movement in Mexico. One of the first and few texts that outline this development is *Against All Odds* by Anna Macías (1982).[16] Much of the feminist critique which comes out of Mexico is published in journals and newspaper supplements such as the popular *Fem* in Mexico City and the supplement to the daily paper *La Jornada* cleverly titled *La doble jornada* (The Double Work Shift) and dedicated to women's lives.

A major contribution to Mexican feminist studies is the extensive bibliography of writer and ambassador Rosario Castellanos. Her *Mujer que sabe latín* presents a series of essays that critique Mexican culture as well as several intellectuals and celebrities. The essay that opens the text, "La mujer y su imagen," makes an important contribution to critical studies on Mexican women and to feminist studies in general. Another study that looks at Mexican feminism in relation to other feminisms is "Feminisms in Latin America," by Nancy Saporta-Sternbach et al.

Until 1848, Chicanas and Mexicanas shared feminist movements.[17] Scholars are attempting to find a defining point that marks the beginning of Chicana/o culture. With the "discovery" of journals, serial novels, and other writing by women from the nineteenth century, many questions will be answered and new light will be shed on issues of identity, politics, and popular culture of the time. Chicanas and Mexicanas have long played an active role in all aspects of political, economic, and cultural life, yet their contributions have often not been part of official history.

An early historical study is Marta Cotera's *Diosa y Hembra* (1976).[18] Other crucial works are Magdalena Mora and Adelaida Del Castillo's *Mexican Woman in the U.S.: Struggles Past and Present* (1990), and Rosaura Sánchez and Rosa Martínez-Cruz's *Essays on la Mujer* (1977). One of the first texts to look at the history and development of Chicana feminism is Marta Cotera's *The Chicana Feminist* (1977); also significant is Alma García's "The Development of Chicana Feminist Discourse, 1970–1980" (1989). Some of the more recent scholarship includes an edited text by Adela de la Torre and Beatriz M. Pesquera, *Building with Our Hands* (1993). Ana Castillo introduces the term "Xicanisma" in opposition to the U.S. feminist movement, which has often ignored the woman of color's struggle. Her collection of essays, *Massacre of the Dreamers* (1994), adds to the development of literature which brings the Chicana's experience to the forefront. Diana Rebolledo's *Women Singing in the Snow* (1995) acts as a theoretical base for Rebolledo and Eliana S. Rivero's *Infinite Divisions* (1993) and is the first analysis of its kind in which the development of a Chicana literary tradition is traced from its roots in 1848 to the present.

Just as Mexicana feminism is often viewed in the context of a larger Latin American feminist discourse, Chicana feminism is viewed in the context of a larger U.S. third world women's feminist discourse. One of the first key texts to offer a discussion of U.S. third world feminism is *This Bridge Called My Back,* edited by Gloria Anzaldúa and Cherríe Moraga (1981). The text which acts as a second volume to *This Bridge Called My Back* is *Making Face, Making Soul,* edited by Gloria Anzaldúa (1990). I also call on the work of Chandra Mohanty et al. for their discussion of third world feminism in *Third World Women and the Politics of Feminism* (1991). These dynamic works offer a critical foundation for examining international feminisms.

Bringing together Chicana and Mexicana feminism presents a tremendous challenge. For the reasons explained above, the two histories have been disconnected in a variety of ways for over a hundred years. Yet, as part of an international feminist community, and particularly a third world feminist community, the two have shared in the same larger struggle for liberation, "not only individual liberation but [one] of social justice and democratization" (Franco, *Plotting Women,* 187). The shared history creates strong ties, ties evident in the contemporary literary expressions of both groups. One important entrance into the literature is by way of the representations of cultural symbols and the mythologies that Chicanas and Mexicanas share.

## MYTHOLOGIES

The re-visioning of myths, legends, and cultural symbols has always been a significant feature of the literature of Chicanas and Mexicanas. Several cultural symbols derive from these myths, the most significant ones dating back to the Spanish conquest of the fifteenth and sixteenth centuries and later adapting to include contemporary events such as the indirect colonization of Mexico and other Latin American countries by the United States, or the internal colonization of Mexicans in the United States. The trilogy of La Virgen de Guadalupe, La

Malinche (also called Malintzin or Marina), and La Llorona has long been present in the literature of Latin America and the Latino United States. As Chicanas and Mexicanas write their experience into history, their literature depicts this corrected history. New archetypes are surfacing in Chicana and Mexicana literature that are replacing or redefining earlier archetypes.

Feminist rereadings of these cultural symbols give these figures agency and often rewrite them as heroines. Of the three figures, La Malinche is the one most grounded in actual Mexican history.[19] She becomes a mythical figure, however, in the patriarchal discourse and is seen as a traitor to her race, the cause of pain and suffering for all generations of Mexicans. Yet, women writers are reclaiming her image, placing Malintzin in her proper historical context and accurately viewing her as a figure of resistance.[20] Norma Alarcón, in "Chicana's Feminist Literature" (1981), begins her argument by stating: "In our patriarchal mythological pantheon, there exists even now a woman who was once real. Her historicity, her experience, her true flesh and blood were discarded" (182). Alarcón, in this essay, gives a critique of how the historical figure of Malintzin has turned into a mythical figure that works toward the continued subjugation of women only if women internalize the myth. Several Chicana writers do refute the myth and have restored the symbol of La Malinche to a woman with agency. While Alarcón critiques the patriarchal system which made La Malinche a slave, she recognizes how women have internalized that myth. She and others argue that La Malinche is the cultural symbol most often called forth and, as such, is the most useful representative for women's rebellion.[21]

The figure of La Llorona, although more prevalent in popular culture than La Malinche, does not always carry the same historical significance. Yet, many view her legend as an adaptation of the myth of La Malinche.[22] La Llorona is a figure in Chicano and Mexican folk legend who, in a supposed moment of insanity, drowned her own children. She wanders the rivers at night searching and calling for them. As is the nature of folk legends, this story has many adaptations, in almost all of which La Llorona is represented as a passive character. Yet, one can also read this story as a cautionary tale, one told to keep children, women, and men in their place. The figure of La Llorona, her history, and the strong cultural significance of her legend are complex. As in the cases of other cultural symbols such as La Malinche and La Virgen de Guadalupe, the symbol of La Llorona is being transformed and reread through the experience of Chicanas and Mexicanas.

José Limón, in "La Llorona" (1986), indicates that prior to his work La Llorona had "received precious little close analytical, interpretive attention in relationship to Greater Mexican society and culture" (69). Limón cites various studies and demonstrates that these do not fully acknowledge the usefulness of La Llorona in feminist interpretation, that they "fall short of a contestative and critical understanding and offer only historically limited, localized interpretations" (73). Quoting the work of Mirandé and Enríquez, he adds: "[La Llorona is] a female who strayed from her proper role as mother, wife, mistress, lover, or patriot . . . a woman who regrets her transgression or bemoans having been denied the fulfillment of her role. . . . La Llorona persists as an image of a woman who willingly or unwillingly fails to comply with feminine imperatives" (70). Límon, indeed, sees the Mirandé and Enríquez reading as passive and offers what he believes to be a more accurate reading. His ethnographic work critiques the vital importance of La Llorona, but it lacks a comprehensive understanding of what he claims are "feminist misreadings" of the Llorona legend.

Giving one cultural symbol precedence over another does not help us toward better understanding. Nonetheless, the work of both critics is important, as important as the work of contemporary poets, novelists, and short story writers who interrogate, appropriate, and revise these cultural symbols so that they become a part of a female interpretation interrupting and disrupting traditional patriarchal modes of thinking.

The third cultural symbol discussed in the present study is the patron saint of Mexico and Latin America, La Virgen de

Guadalupe. In poetic form, Gloria Anzaldúa retells the story of La Virgen's divine appearance:

El nueve de diciembre del año 1531
a las cuatro de la madrugada
un pobre indio que se llamaba Juan Diego
iba cruzando el cerro de Tepeyac
cuando oyó un canto de pájaro.
Alzó al [sic] cabeza vio que en la cima del cerro
estaba cubierta con una brillante nube blanca.
Parada en frente del sol
sobre una luna creciente
sostenida por un ángel
estaba una azteca
vestida en ropa de india.
Nuestra Señora María de Coatlalopeuh
se le apareció
"Juan Diegito [sic], El-que-habla-como-un-águila,"
La Virgen le dijo en el lenguaje azteca.
"Para hacer mi altar este cerro eligo [sic].
Dile a tu gente que yo soy la madre de Dios,
a los indios yo les ayudaré."
Estó [sic] se lo contó a Juan Zumarraga [sic]
pero el obispo no le creyo [sic].
Juan Diego volvió, lleno su tilma
con rosas de castilla
creciendo milagrosamente en la nieve.
Se las llevó al obispo,
y cuando abrió su tilma
el retrato de La Virgen
ahí estaba pintado.
[On the ninth of December, 1531,
at four o'clock in the morning
a poor Indian named Juan Diego
was crossing the hill of Tepeyac
when he heard a bird singing.
He looked up and saw that the top of the hill
was covered with a brilliant white cloud.

Standing in front of the sun
on a crescent moon
supported by an angel
was an Aztec woman
dressed in Indian clothes.
Our Lady Mary of Coatlalopeuh
had appeared to him
"Juan Dieguito [sic], He-who-speaks-like-an-eagle,"
The Virgin said to him in the Aztec language.
"I have chosen this hill for the making of my altar.
Tell your people that I am the Mother of God,
I will help the Indians."
He told this to Juan Zumárraga
but the bishop did not believe him.
Juan Diego returned, filled his blanket
with roses of Castile
growing miraculously in the snow.
He took them to the bishop,
and when he opened his blanket
the portrait of the Virgin
was painted there.] (*Borderlands/La Frontera*, 28)[23]

Although in patriarchal culture La Virgen de Guadalupe
has been viewed as the pure figure in the virgin/whore dichot-
omy, women and men have seen her as a symbol of resistance
and cultural survival. During the conquest, when the native
people of Mexico were supposedly being Christianized, they
were still seen as "savages" not worthy of full membership in
the church. Yet La Virgen de Guadalupe appeared to an Indian
man, Juan Diego, to express her and God's servitude to his
people. A brown virgin represented acceptance of the native
peoples by their newly adopted God. Some scholars, however,
speculate that La Virgen was fundamentally an adaptation by
the indigenous tribe of their earth goddess, Tonantzin. In this
reading, La Virgen would be a symbol of resistance to the con-
queror's religion. Syncretism is evident throughout history as
the Catholic Church tried and continues trying to impose its
beliefs on the people of the Americas.

Mexicana and Chicana cultural critics and writers are highly invested in claiming a space in the rewriting and reconstruction of history. It is a necessary bond that must continue to be formed and maintained between those who embody the geographical border.

## CHAPTER SUMMARIES

The present work opens with an examination of and theoretical approaches to Chicana literature that sets it within the context of the literature by other U.S. women of color. Eurocentric readings, readings that privilege western tradition over nonwestern tradition, are often narrow because of a lack of understanding of the sociohistorical realities of Chicanas. I compare such readings with how Chicana/o theorists read Chicana literature and those who look at past and present theoretical approaches to the field.

After exploring the roots of Chicana literature from the multiple contexts of cultural, historical, and geographical borders, I discuss the experimentation with genre that takes place in these border zones of Mexicana and Chicana literature. "Marginal" literatures often employ marginal forms. Several Chicana writers employ nontraditional genres to express their narratives, writing short stories or fragmented forms rather than the novels long considered the highest form of literature. Chicana writers, already marginalized by virtue of their ethnicity and gender, risk further marginalization when they choose to use experimental forms. Nonetheless, the decision to break from traditional genres is often another strategy of resistance for these writers.

In some cases, that of Sandra Cisneros, for example, publishers have embraced Chicana literature, thereby increasing the likelihood of other Chicanas being published by mainstream presses. One must ask, though, how certain writers are selected to be mainstream and other are not. Those whose works are not published by mainstream presses struggle to have their production distributed to a general audience, and all too often Chicana literature is read only in academic courses.

Chapters 2, 3, and 4 examine modes of resistance used by Chicana and Mexicana writers to overcome the confinements of gender and sexual oppression. This resistance is integral to the theoretical discourse of these writers. Along with resisting a male-dominated culture, these writers reshape cultural symbols that have been prevalent in Chicano and Mexican literature.

Chapter 2 addresses the work of Sandra Cisneros by focusing on two texts: *The House on Mango Street* (1988) and "Woman Hollering Creek" (1990). A critical reading of these texts demonstrates the ways in which Cisneros transforms various cultural symbols to serve her particular political/theoretical agenda.

Chapter 3 examines the works of Mexicana writers Carmen Boullosa and Laura Esquivel. A close examination of Boullosa's poetry and prose reveals how she redefines family institutions and undermines patriarchy in the process. Through creation of a new cultural symbol, which she names "La Salvaja," Boullosa provides honest, uncensored insight into what it is to be female in a male-dominated society. Laura Esquivel's woman-centered narrative, *Como agua para chocolate* (1989), on the other hand, presents us with other modes of resistance and modes of rebellion. Chapter 4 concentrates on the work of Helena María Viramontes.

Cisneros, Boullosa, Esquivel, and Viramontes involve themselves in redefining and transforming family institutions, critiquing patriarchy in the larger culture and within their own communities, collectivizing certain relevant cultural symbols, and questioning harmful dualisms. For example, in "Woman Hollering Creek," Cisneros transforms the traditionally passive portrayal of La Llorona into a strong figure of resistance. Viramontes, in "Cariboo Café," presents a collective La Llorona that refers to larger social and economic issues: by portraying a poor, undocumented washerwoman from Central America, her tragic experience with the *contras* in her country, and her heartbreaking encounter with the police in the United States, Viramontes disrupts the geographical border and makes us see how an international feminism is possible.[24] The narratives explored in this chapter also reflect the influence of the family and present family units not typically portrayed in mainstream literature. Unlike narratives that assume a "traditional male-headed household," which does not exist, these works present a historical reality.[25] In Viramontes's short story "The Moths," a grandmother and granddaughter constitute the safe and loving family unit. "Neighbors" also questions the idea of home and family, borders and boundaries.

Scrutinizing these works raises broader literary and cultural questions. Are Cisneros, Viramontes, Esquivel, and Boullosa, even as they resist the traditional notions of cultural symbols, perpetuating the negative stereotypes that these symbols have represented in the past? How are these cultural symbols manipulated and for what purpose? Often, their representations are appropriated by non-Chicanas and non-Mexicanas and result in further exploitation of a culture they do not know. Appropriation of these symbols is becoming more worrisome with the awakening of a new "multicultural consciousness," which often becomes another path to pluralization. Who becomes invested in these symbols and why? Are new cultural symbols actually displacing traditional symbols in the works of these writers? Representations of cultural icons that are ingrained in the social consciousness of a people will not happen in a short period of time. However, by offering a revision of these female symbols or by attempting to portray a more accurate historical account, as in the case of La Malinche, an effort to end the perpetuation of negative representations of womanhood begins.[26]

Mexicana and Chicana writers are highly invested in these projects and, through their narratives, are reimagining history. The woman-centered consciousness that their literature evokes speaks to the long tradition of feminism. Third world feminism is still often marginalized, and theories and practices from these movements are not often seen as valid forms. This work will demonstrate how works by Mexicanas and Chicanas presents a political and theoretical agenda undermining the patriarchy and calling for coalitions across borders.

# CROSSING BORDERS AND BLURRING BOUNDARIES: SANDRA CISNEROS RE-VISIONS THE WAILING WOMAN

Chapter 1 discusses the early work of Chicana feminist critics as well as more recent significant scholarship by Chicana critics. When analyzing these critics' work as a whole, the following political/theoretical projects may be seen: (1) a redefinition and transformation of family institutions;[1] (2) a critique of the patriarchy in the dominant culture and in Chicanas' own communities; (3) a collectivization of certain relevant cultural symbols; (4) an interrogation of harmful dualisms; and (5) an examination of issues of identity (especially sexual identity) and subjectivity.[2] The fiction I invoke in this analysis is in dialogue with this project.

One of the first published collective articulations by women of color in the United States to question the systems that have subordinated women is *This Bridge Called My Back*.[3] Gloria Anzaldúa and Cherríe Moraga stress that theory for women of color is articulated through their particular ethnic and cultural experience; furthermore, the authors see writing as a "tool for self-preservation and revolution" (xiii). In *Bridge*, many contributors stress that theory needs to be viewed as personal as well as political. Through their political writing, these authors talk back to the patriarchal systems and the elitism of the academy. Not surprisingly, they challenge the feminist movement to look at its classism and racism. The authors' feminist political theory derives from their lived experience, and a new brand of feminism has evolved: feminism on the border, or bridge feminism.[4]

In *Making Face, Making Soul*, Gloria Anzaldúa offers her own definition and application of theory: "Thus we need *teorías* that will enable us to interpret what happens in the world, that will explain how and why we relate to certain people in specific ways, that will reflect what goes on between inner, outer and peripheral 'I's within a person and between the personal 'I's and collective 'we' of our ethnic communities" (xxv). The blurring of boundaries between theory and lived experience is of primary importance in the theoretical model that Anzaldúa proposes; she insists that theorists and theory be responsive and responsible to the community.

The root of theory, "theor," is defined as "one who travels in order to see things, also an envoy, ambassador."[5] Anzaldúa, then, does not stray from the original meaning of theory, but, rather, embraces it within her own critique and encourages her audience to do the same. Furthermore, she racializes its meaning to make it meaningful to the women-of-color politics she is promoting. She reminds us that we need to look at personal experiences in order to articulate them with new theoretical models and to bring them into the larger community, not only into the academy. These models provide a more organic means of interpreting individual experience.

In Anzaldúa's adapted definition, then, theory by women of color would be found in unconventional places, since hegemonic culture often considers the work of women of color illegitimate. As Sonia Saldívar-Hull suggests: "Hegemony has so constructed the idea of method and theory that often we cannot recognize anything that is different from what the dominant discourse constructs. We have to look in nontraditional places for our theories: in the prefaces to anthologies, in the interstices of autobiographies, in our cultural artifacts, our *cuentos*" ("Feminism on the Border," 206). The political/theoretical agenda for women of color, as Saldívar-Hull suggests, is often embedded in their narrative texts.

Certainly, other writers maintain similar agendas; however, because of the subject position of women of color, issues of race and class are often inherent in their literature. Specifically recalling Anzaldúa's *Borderlands/La Frontera*, Saldívar-Hull notes: "Feminism on the border exists in a borderland not limited to geographic space, a feminism that resides in a space not acknowledged by hegemonic culture" ("Feminism on the

Border," 211). Women of color are articulating a literature of resistance.

Repeatedly in the work of Chicana writer Sandra Cisneros, we see these border feminism projects being carried out, beginning with her first book of vignettes, published in 1984, and continuing with *Woman Hollering Creek and Other Stories.*[6] In 1985, *The House on Mango Street* was awarded the Before Columbus Foundation's American Book Award. In the book, Cisneros portrays her protagonist Esperanza Cordero as a young rebel coming of age in her mostly Latino barrio in Chicago. These stories, although written from a child's point of view, display the resistant nature of Cisneros's narrator, who rebels against the oppression that she faces as a child growing up in poverty and against the cultural oppression that she faces as a female. The "protection" that the culture imposes on Chicanas shelters her and encourages her to keep silent on certain taboo subjects, namely, sexuality. Because patriarchy is still a powerful force in Chicano culture, Chicanas are always at risk when they write against that tradition.[7]

## THE HOUSE ON MANGO STREET

When Cisneros produces her narrative, she is rewriting the way that women and particularly Chicanas have traditionally been portrayed in literature. To write about a girl's coming-of-age, Cisneros first must rewrite the story of the woman-child. She writes about Esperanza the child as an empowered being, independent and strong enough to live in the world on her own, independent of a man. Because the story takes place in the space of only one year, Esperanza is still an adolescent at the conclusion, yet her experiences allow her to imagine her future as a woman.

## Method

Cisneros, writing from her particular experience as a Chicana, goes beyond a simple rewriting of the female experience to include her cultural experience: not only has the Chicana been a victim of distorted portrayals, but Chicana/o culture as a whole has been treated in the same manner. Cisneros gives voice to her culture as she retells tradition; she rewrites herself using Esperanza's child's voice.

As Chicanas rewrite their history, they also devise new forms that allow them to speak in the voice that best relates their experience. This step is necessary; because Chicanas' experiences may not conform to traditional forms, they must rewrite or reinvent traditional male genres. In *Mango Street,* a new form is created; placing this form into any one particular genre, however, is a difficult task. Cisneros explains that she "wanted to write stories that were a cross between poetry and fiction." Other times, she calls them vignettes, or "lazy poems" (Olivares, "Sandra Cisneros' *The House on Mango Street,*" 160, 161). This genre gives Cisneros the freedom to tell her story using the voice she feels most comfortable with; she does not feel obligated to confine herself to any one traditional genre. With a child's words and playfulness, she tells a sophisticated story of Esperanza's journey into adulthood. By using a child's voice, the author is speaking to the developing child, the adolescent. Yet, the child's voice becomes a beguiling tool. As a child Esperanza can get away with her critique of patriarchy. The wisdom she imparts to women seems more like a grandmother's wisdom.

## Writing

Esperanza's medium for her coming-of-age process, a female bildungsroman, is, of course, writing. For Esperanza, writing is more than a means of telling her story; it is an act of self-discovery and self-creation. These acts are first encouraged by an aunt lying on her deathbed: "You must remember to keep writing, Esperanza. You must keep writing. It will keep you free, and I said yes, but at that time I didn't know what she meant. . . . And then she died, my aunt who listened to my poems. And then we began to dream the dreams" (*House on Mango Street,* 60; all quotations in the text are from this edition). The freedom her aunt speaks of is literal, for Esperanza's writing will take her away from the harsh world in which she lives; as we can infer from the conclusion, it will gain her a formal education. Yet, her dreams are not focused on her material reality. Her dream is a house of her own and the ability to live by her own rules, and not a man's. To write and "dream the dreams"(57), Esperanza must come to terms with her world. She must acknowledge, though not accept, the world that she lives in with all of its poverty and oppression. As a young woman of color, an acceptance of the societal role prescribed for her will mean her demise.

## Poverty

Esperanza needs to see the reality of her world before she can take steps to change her destiny and that of those less fortunate, those who do not have her tools to escape their poverty, which is maintained by racism and patriarchy. Her challenge is two-fold: as a Chicana, she rebels against racism; and as a female, she rebels against the male power structure in her community. Although the poverty she lives in is linked mostly to class op-pression, sexual oppression also plays a tremendous role. In any patriarchal culture, a woman's sexuality is not her own.

Esperanza is disillusioned by all that surrounds her, and she often finds her own way of breaking away from her oppres-sion. In "A House of My Own," she imagines a pure space where no person or thing can harm her.[8] In "Born Bad," she writes poems that help her to "dream the dreams":

I want to be
like the waves on the sea,
like the clouds in the wind,
but I'm me.
One day I'll jump
out of my skin.
I'll shake the sky
like a hundred violins." (56)

Esperanza takes great risks in rebelling against her world. By doing so, she may lose a "legitimate" position in her culture: the role of wife and mother. Marriage and motherhood are still valued as a woman's greatest vocation. However, she is determined not to adopt the generational suffering of the women in her family:[9]

> My great-grandmother. I would've liked to have known her, a wild horse of a woman, so wild she wouldn't marry until my great-grandfather threw a sack over her head and carried her off. Just like that, as if she were a fancy chandelier. That's the way he did it.
>
> And the story goes she never forgave him. She looked out the window all her life, the way so many women sit their sadness on an elbow. I wonder if she made the best with what she got or was she sorry because she couldn't be all the things she wanted to be. Esperanza. I have inherited her name, but I don't want to inherit her place by the window. (12)

Esperanza accepts the images fed to her by television; she accepts the picture of the American Dream held by her parents. She is convinced that she will move into the house she has always dreamed of, one "like the houses on T.V." (8). When she is disappointed once again by where she has to live, she becomes more determined to have a house of her own one day, a house that will not embarrass her and, more important, a place where she can feel liberated.

## Constructing a House of Her Own

When Esperanza lists the many places that she has lived, she ends by saying: "And before that I can't remember. But what I remember most is moving a lot" (7). More than a sign of success or poverty, however, having a real house means security and stability to Esperanza; her present house only reflects her view of herself, her poverty, and her shame. As Ramón Saldívar reminds us: "In 'A House of My Own,' Cisneros' narrator echoes the feminist plea for 'a room of one's own' as a site of poetic self-creation" (*Chicano Narrative,* 183). Later, as Esperanza writes a new house for herself, she also rewrites her identity, forming an escape to a world where she has control.

She has been moving all of her life; none of these places is home. The house on Mango Street is just a house to Esperanza, not a home. The street name, however, carries positive connotations, for the mango is a symbol of cultural survival.[10] Because she has grown up in cold, urban Chicago, the mango is a rare, precious, and expensive commodity for her. A symbol of the tropics and of Mexico, the fruit elicits nostalgia in city dwellers. The mango, like Esperanza and her four skinny trees, seems out of place: "They are the only ones who understand me. I am the only one who understands them. Four skinny trees with skinny necks and pointy elbows like mine. Four who do not belong here but are here" (71). Esperanza appreciates how the trees are able to adapt to their environment and grow strong, even though they are firmly planted in the earth. Thomas Friedman, in *The Lexus and the Olive Tree*, notes that trees "represent everything that roots us, identifies us and locates us in the world—whether it be belonging to a family, a community, a tribe, a nation, a religion, or, most of all, a place called home" (27). While Esperanza's ancestry may be linked to the land, she is quite displaced. She has been replanted somewhere foreign and uninviting.

But Esperanza's hope does not cover her shame—shame for not having a home she can point to, shame for everything that reveals her poverty and oppression. Even her name, which means "hope," is a source of disappointment and shame: "I would like to baptize myself under a new name, a name more like the real me, the one nobody sees. Esperanza as Lisandra or Maritza or Zeze the X. Yes. Something like Zeze the X will do" (13). For Esperanza, her name has only sad connotations. It is a dark and sad name, an expression of her poverty and homelessness. Because it was her great-grandmother's name, it is linked to the male-dominated tradition of her culture, and in this story she wants to re-create herself by baptizing herself with a new name. Neither her culture nor her family would be able to define a name like "Zeze the X." She does not want a name associated with the generations of women suffering as quiet rebels, sitting by the window, their anger silenced. Surrounded by the poverty of her class, she is nonetheless hopeful that she will leave Mango Street someday. She is her name, and she later discovers that she is also Mango Street.

However, this reclamation of her name and her home does not come until much later, when she is more willing to accept her reality and how capable she is of changing it. She cannot erase the year that she has been living on Mango Street; all the experiences will become a part of her. Later, this experience becomes her creative self, for it is from this year on Mango Street that she is able to rewrite herself. Her writing equals her liberation; she wages her own quiet war in which her personal weapons are paper and pen.

## Sexual Awakening

Esperanza's liberation also includes a sexual awakening. As she and her friends play jump rope in "Hips," Esperanza says: "One day you wake up and they [hips] are there. Ready and waiting like a new Buick with the keys in the ignition. Ready to take you where?" (47). In this story, she takes pride in her hips and says that she is obviously the only one who can speak with any authority on the matter. Esperanza and her playmates explain all of the reasons one must have hips; hips are something that they all look forward to. This game expresses the girls' curiosity about women's bodies and their own development.

As Esperanza recognizes the changes in her body, she also recognizes other aspects of growing up. The children's games in "The Monkey Garden" bring her to this awareness:

> Who was it that said I was getting too old to play the games? Who was it I didn't listen to? I only remember that when the others ran, I wanted to run too, up and down and through the monkey garden, fast as the boys . . .
>
> I looked at my feet in their white socks and ugly round shoes. They seemed far away. They didn't seem to be my feet anymore. And the garden that had been such a good place to play didn't seem mine either. (89)

Compared with the Garden of Eden, a garden of heavenly and earthly delight, this garden is a site of oppression and violation for Esperanza and the other girls. Like the Garden of Eden, it is the location of Esperanza's loss of innocence. A garden in the middle of the city might be considered an oasis by some, but for Esperanza the monkey garden is a wasteland.

Rebelling against growing up, and expressing her sadness at losing her childhood, Esperanza is also witnessing the different relationships that girls and boys have as they become women and men. She expresses frustration with this change. The boys are in control in the garden, and Esperanza resents this, though she still does not have the language to express her intuition:

> I don't know why, but something inside me wanted to throw a stick. Something wanted to say no when I watched Sally going into the garden with Tito's buddies all grinning. It was just a kiss, that's all. A kiss for each one. So what, she said.
>
> Only how come I felt angry inside. Like something wasn't right. (89)

Esperanza is the only person in this story who sees anything wrong with this game invented by one of the boys, where each boy demands a kiss in order for Sally to retrieve her keys. The boys have all been socialized to believe that it is natural for them to use Sally for their own pleasure; even Sally sees nothing wrong with it. And since this behavior has been normalized, Esperanza has difficulty understanding her anger. This anger leads her to reevaluate her ideas about sexuality. She becomes suspicious of the relationships between boys and girls who learn their roles at an early age. Esperanza realizes early on that "the boys and girls live in separate worlds. The boys in their universe and we in ours" (11).

In other vignettes, she examines differences between these two worlds and how they affect her. Sally is "dangerously beautiful"; Marin waits for a man to come and change her life; Alicia inherits her mama's rolling pin and sleepiness; and Esperanza's own great-grandmother has inherited a place by the window—all of which Esperanza rejects. In rejecting "a place by the window," she writes about the generational suffering and about herself and a place away from the window, removed from what has been the fate of other women in her life. She refuses to share in the repression of self that they have suffered, because she realizes that she has other options.

One of Esperanza's most outwardly rebellious acts is seen when she acts like a man, in "Beautiful and Cruel":

> [B]ut I have decided not to grow up tame like the others who lay their necks on the threshold waiting for the ball and chain.
>
> I have begun my own quiet war. Simple. Sure. I am the one who leaves the table like a man, without putting back the chair or picking up the plate. (82)

Though on the surface this seems a relatively safe rebellion for a child, her opposition in this story comes from her frustration with a certain aspect of her society. Surely, it will be her mother or another woman in the home who will pick up her plate when Esperanza leaves the table "like a man." Her rebellion means the oppression of other women.

Esperanza's understanding of rebellion is "simple, sure," and certainly naïve, pointing to an interesting dilemma that is not specific to her position. In reality, the girl child, by her act of doing domestic chores, makes less work for the mother or other women in the family. In a traditional family such as Esperanza's, the brothers or the father would not share the domestic work. Behaving "like a man" places Esperanza in a double bind. With this behavior, she cannot improve her own situation without making that of the other women worse. If she truly wishes to participate in a rebellion that will benefit all girls and women and not just herself, she must come to an understanding of the consequences of her actions.[11]

In this rebellion lies Esperanza's rejection of the institution of marriage, for she sees how in marriage women are traditionally dominated. She wants to rewrite her destiny, and in a later story commits herself to single life. For Esperanza, coming of age involves these "simple acts," and this quiet rebellion is part of the process of making sense of her world and her place in it.

Nonetheless, the decision is a radical one—marriage is a strong tradition in Esperanza's culture. She rejects this tradition because she has seen "bad things" happen to married women, and she does not want the same fate. The married women in her life are battered, lonely, and abandoned. Esperanza recognizes her mother's unhappiness in being unable to use her talents to achieve her dreams. Esperanza recognizes very clearly her "own quiet war," knowing that, for her own safety, she must practice silent acts of daily resistance.

In the same way that Esperanza grows up with mythical notions of the American Dream, she also sees and embraces the romantic notions of love that she has received from television and from her friend Sally. This picture is distorted for her, and she experiences the sometimes tragic consequences of sexual awareness in "Red Clowns": "Sally, you lied. It wasn't what you said at all. What he did. Where he touched me. I didn't want it, Sally. The way they said it, the way it's supposed to be, all the storybooks and movies, why did you lie to me?" (93). This first sexual encounter is a horrifying experience for Esperanza, and she says to Sally at the end of the story: "I don't remember. It was dark. I don't remember. I don't remember. Please don't make me tell it all" (93). This allows us to see the horror of this experience: the loss of innocence, rape. Esperanza wants neither to remember nor to tell this story. Her shame and embarrassment about the violation are related to the family stories she has heard; she does not want to be seen as a "bad woman."

## Leaving Mango Street

Although Esperanza is rewriting the Chicana's position throughout the entire text, after this violation, she becomes more determined to make her own reality, to write about her own life as removed from any patriarchal structure. After this story, she focuses on leaving Mango Street and acquiring a house of her own. She no longer believes in the stories of her childhood, or the storybook images. By living an independent life, she will change the tradition that has kept her and other women silent:

> Not a flat. Not an apartment in back. Not a man's house. Not a daddy's. A house all my own. With my porch and my pillow, my pretty purple petunias. My books and my stories. My two shoes waiting beside the bed. Nobody to shake a stick at. Nobody's garbage to pick up after.
>
> Only a house quiet as snow, a space for myself to go, clean as paper before the poem. (100)

The house in the early part of the text may have been only a symbol of her escape from her poverty; now it has become more a part of her as she redefines it, rewrites it to include what she wants in a home all her own. If she can leave her male-dominated environment and live her life of independence, she will be freer to invent the kind of life she wants. She becomes a character in Chicana literature that breaks the silence.

Esperanza's empowerment is her writing. As she writes down her thoughts and examines her world through writing, she discovers that "the ghost does not ache so much" (101). The ghost is the haunting conditions of her life as a Chicana. Her writing allows her the freedom to define herself and express the issues that she can otherwise not speak out about. In the beginning, Esperanza is desperate to escape her oppressive reality; toward the end, with the help of friends, she realizes that she cannot deny who she is. She tells Alicia: "I don't belong. I don't ever want to come from here." But Alicia responds: "Like it or not you are Mango Street and one day you'll come back too" (98). Esperanza cannot deny the experiences, good or bad, that now shape her identity. As a Chicana writer, the responsibility of coming home is connected to the writing process.

Seeing the world through different eyes, this world that she once wished to deny becomes the source of her creativity. Writing is important for her and for other women; for her it symbolizes education and an opportunity to "be somebody." Her family tries to protect her from the world, but her daily life requires her to see the "real" world in her small space of Mango Street. Although telling her story may be difficult, Esperanza accepts the challenge, thereby giving girls and women a voice by recording their lives and retelling their history. She is tempted to forget who she is, to escape her reality and create a whole new life for herself while forgetting Mango Street, but people remind her of her responsibility. When she is granted a wish by "the three sisters," they read her mind as they tell her: "When you leave you must remember to come back for the others. A circle, understand? You will always be Esperanza. You will always be Mango Street. You can't erase what you know: You can't forget who you are" (98). Esperanza realizes that these sisters have magical powers: they have read her mind and they know of what she dreams. This sisterhood links her in a positive way to her community and to women who have found their own liberation. She can dismiss their words or she can accept their challenge.

She chooses to accept the challenge and makes her experience the collective experience of Chicanas and other women who have not been given the privilege of writing their story. She rewrites the women's experience and her community's experience as well.

Because she speaks with the voice of a child, Esperanza appears innocent about many things. Examining her more closely, we see that she has an acute perception and sensitivity. In simple terms, she analyzes the complex world around her where people are surviving despite the oppression they experience. In the story "Mango Says Goodbye Sometimes," she speaks of "a girl who didn't want to belong." In this story, we see the growth that has taken place during her year on Mango Street:

> One day I will pack my bags of books and paper. One day I will say goodbye to Mango. I am too strong for her to keep me here forever. One day I will go away.
>
> Friends and neighbors will say, What happened to that Esperanza? Where did she go with all those books and paper? Why did she march so far away?
>
> They will not know I have gone away to come back. For the ones I left behind. For the ones who cannot get out. (101–102)

By the end of the book, Esperanza has completely rewritten herself and retold the history of a young girl's struggle to define her own life. By leaving Mango Street, Esperanza places herself in another physical space in order to give her story a place of importance; she has rewritten for herself a home where she will have the freedom to tell her story outside of the confines of a patriarchal culture. Her ultimate decision to return to her community with new educational tools demonstrates her commitment to creating new liberating places not only for herself, but also for her community.

Cisneros rejects the traditional role of woman and female writer by telling the stories that have long been forbidden to women; she dares to deal with issues of childhood and sexuality through the voice of Esperanza, through Esperanza's coming-of-age in the community that she rewrites for herself. Indeed, Cisneros rewrites history by giving the woman-child a voice and a space to tell her story. As Rita Sánchez words it: "Writing, breaking the silence, subjective as it may appear, becomes a monumental and collective act because it signifies overcoming, freeing oneself from the confines and conditions of history" ("Chicana Writer Breaking Out of Silence," 3). For Esperanza, writing is a way out; it is what Cisneros articulates in a *New York Times* interview when she states that there is a power in "making people think in a different way" (Tabor, "At the Library with Sandra Cisneros," B2).

As is evident in the vignette that ends the narrative, "Mango Says Goodbye Sometimes," Esperanza knows she is strong and able to overcome the obstacles of her poverty. It is a child's way of defining power: leaving in order to come back "for the ones [she] left behind" (102). She will return to educate her friends and neighbors; by doing so, she will have empowered herself.

## "WOMAN HOLLERING CREEK"

In Cisneros's second short story collection, *Woman Hollering Creek and Other Stories*, the author creates a narrative in which she further critiques the issues she raises in *The House on Mango Street*. She transforms traditional cultural symbols into figures of resistance for women, and the implications of this strategy form her theories.

Cisneros takes part in creating theory by rewriting the symbols and therefore rewriting a history that has denied or ignored women's contributions. With a revision of history comes a revision of the theoretical constructs that have informed that history. Her characters are battered women, abused children, undocumented workers, and girl-rebels. In *Woman Hollering Creek*, Cisneros raises issues of women's economic dependence on their husbands and violence against women. She then presents communities of women and figures of resistance as alternatives to the culturally accepted oppression that her characters face.

The title story, "Woman Hollering Creek," depicts one type of resistance through an experimental narrative form. The opening of the story is reminiscent of a *telenovela*, or soap opera. Cisneros evokes this form by beginning her story as a soap opera would begin. The women of the small town are looking for glamour and living vicariously through their *novela* heroines: "*Tú o nadie*. 'You or No One.' The title of the current favorite *telenovela*. The beautiful Lucía Méndez having to put up with all kinds of hardships of the heart, separation and betrayal, and loving always loving no matter what, because *that* is the most important thing, and did you see Lucía Méndez on the Bayer aspirin commercials—wasn't she lovely? Does she dye her hair do you think? Cleófilas is going to go to the *farmacia* and buy a hair rinse; her girlfriend Chela will apply it—it's not that difficult at all" (44).

As a popular television form, the *telenovela* is accessible to Cleófilas, the working-class protagonist. Cleófilas and her friends are strongly influenced by the consumer culture presented on television, which inspires dreams of acquiring their own glamourous lives. When Don Serafín gives "permission to Juan Pedro Martínez to take Cleófilas Enriqueta DeLeón Hernández as his bride, across her father's threshold, over several miles of dirt road and several miles of paved, over one border and beyond to a town *en el otro lado*—on the other side"(43), Cleófilas's own soap opera begins. She looks forward to the fulfillment of the American Dream, but very soon after their move, she becomes disillusioned by her reality: a life of abuse perpetrated by her own husband.

Cleófilas discovers her life with her husband to be a soap opera, "only now the episodes got sadder. And there were no commercials in between for comic relief. And no happy ending in sight" (*Woman Hollering Creek*, 52–53; all quotations in the text are from this edition). Her relationship with her husband is nothing like she had hoped. She dreams of a greater romance:

> But what Cleófilas has been waiting for, has been whispering and sighing and giggling for, has been anticipating since she was old enough to lean against the window displays of gauze and butterflies and lace, is passion. Not the kind on the cover of the *¡Alarma!* magazines mind you, where the lover is photographed with the bloody fork she used to salvage her good name. But passion in its purest crystaline essence. The kind the books and songs and *telenovelas* describe when one finds, finally, the great love of one's life, and does whatever one can, must do, at whatever the cost. (44)

Taking her cue from the protagonists of popular narratives and the *telenovelas*, Cleófilas does what many women in her situation do: she tolerates the abuse and suffers for love, "because to suffer for love is good. The pain all sweet somehow. In the end" (45). Yet, she realizes the pain is not so sweet when her romance turns sour immediately after her marriage, when she is physically and emotionally abused by her husband and when none of her *telenovela* dreams come true.

Nor do other Chicana protagonists, including many of Cisneros's characters in *The House on Mango Street,* see a way out of abusive homes, and so they remain. However, in "Woman Hollering Creek," Cisneros gives her female protagonist new options. This is part of her theorizing method: making women aware of their situation and offering them new options for living as independent and powerful people. If it is true, as Anzaldúa states, that "theory produces effects that change people and the way they perceive the world," then Cisneros is producing this in her fiction by presenting "different ways of seeing" for her female protagonists.[12]

Another way that Cisneros changes perceptions is through the rewriting and reimagining of the Llorona folk legend, which begins the second section of "Woman Hollering Creek." La Llorona (wailing woman) in this story becomes La Gritona (hollering woman). Each of these names carries specific connotations. By referring to the mythic La Llorona and examining the cultural implications of this figure, Cisneros shows us even more clearly the radical difference in these two names. As explicated in the previous chapter, La Llorona has often been represented as a woman without agency.[13] She has been portrayed simply as a crazy woman who drowned her children and cries in repentance for her act. In other versions of the Llorona legend, however, she is seen as a representation of Mexico after the conquest and of La Malinche, crying for her conquered land and children. In each of these versions, she is crying and powerless.

Like La Llorona, La Gritona is an outcast, a type of woman who would not be accepted easily by everyone because she is seen as evil. She is more similar to La Llorona than different from her. Yet, Cisneros gives La Gritona a powerful image, both in her representation as the creek and in her personification as Felice. The creek that runs behind Cleófilas's new house in Seguin, Texas, is called La Gritona, but nobody is sure why the creek was given this name: "*La Gritona.* Such a funny name for such a lovely arroyo. But that's what they called the creek that ran behind the house. Though no one could say whether the woman had hollered from anger or pain. The natives only knew the arroyo you crossed on the way to San Antonio, and then once again on the way back, was called Woman Hollering, a name no one from these parts questioned, much less understood" (44).

Cleófilas is interested in this creek and adopts it as her friend. The creek carries the dual image of drowning and rebirth. In her monotonous life, the only comfort Cleófilas has at times is the creek. Cleófilas can choose the company of the creek or that of her neighbors, Soledad or Dolores.

Cisneros's characters all have names appropriate to their personality and lifestyle. Soledad, which translates literally as "loneliness" or "solitude," "likes to call herself a widow, though how she came to be one was a mystery. Her husband had either died, or run away with an ice-house floozie, or simply gone out for cigarettes one afternoon and never came back" (46). The neighbor Dolores, whose name translates as "pain" or "grief," has a house which "smelled too much of incense and candles from the altars that burned continuously in memory of two sons who had died in the last war and one husband who had died shortly after from grief" (47).

Cleófilas, who is becoming more independent, is not offered support by her neighbors. She chooses the creek; she decides to be less dependent on her husband and to turn her attention to strong women and to La Llorona, who by now is La Gritona. Once Cleófilas begins to recognize the power of the creek and the positive effect it has on her, she no longer sees La Llorona as the image she has carried with her since childhood. Rather, she sees the creek as her salvation and opportunity for rebirth. Cleófilas comes to see that the personified creek can offer her more comfort than her husband can; she gains peace from it, whereas she only experiences abuse and neglect from her husband. The creek is her dependable friend and brings her feelings of solitude. It also inspires childhood memories: "In the springtime, the creek is a good-size alive thing with a voice all its own, all day and all night calling in its high, silver voice. Is it *La Llorona,* the weeping woman? *La Llorona,* who drowned her own children. Perhaps *La Llorona* is the one they named the creek after, she thinks, remembering all the stories she learned as a child" (51). The women of the town warn her of the harm that La Gritona can bring her: "Don't go out there after dark, *mi'jita.* Stay near the house. *No es bueno para la salud. Mala suerte.* Bad luck. *Mal aire.* You'll get sick and the baby too. You'll catch a fright wandering about in the dark, and then you'll see how right we were" (51).

Soledad and Dolores become patriarchy's gatekeepers. When they warn Cleófilas to "stay near the house," they are also cautioning her to remain within the confined role that her culture and society at large has dictated for her. The neighbor women need her to validate their lives.

Cleófilas must be special to have been summoned by the seductive creek. Had Dolores or Soledad ever been called by the creek, they would not have heard it because they have accepted their lives as weeping widows. Cleófilas is still young enough and willing enough to change her destiny. She disregards her neighbors. She is not afraid to take her chances with "catching a fright." As she sits beside the creek with her baby, Cleófilas wonders if the quiet and the loneliness that she experiences is what "drives a woman to the darkness under the trees" (51). Sitting under the trees should bring her solace, but like Esperanza in *The House on Mango Street,* Cleófilas is displaced. She has a house, but it is not a home.

Unlike La Llorona, who kills her children, Cleófilas is saving her children's lives and her own by taking them away from an abusive father and environment. While she is washing dishes one day, a conversation between her husband and his friends inspires her to reflect on her life of domestic abuse: "Was Cleófilas just exaggerating as her husband always said? It seemed the newspapers were full of such stories. This woman found on the side of the interstate. This one pushed from a moving car. This one's cadaver, this one unconscious, this one beaten blue. Her ex-husband, her husband, her lover, her father, her brother, her uncle, her friend, her co-worker. Always. The same grisly news in the pages of the dailies. She dunked a glass under the soapy water for a moment—shivered" (52).

Water in the traditional La Llorona tales is a negative image, because the madwoman kills her children by drowning them in the river. With the shift to La Gritona, the water becomes cleansing and therapeutic, as represented in the above passage.[14] The water is also a continual reminder of Cleófilas's slow process of rebirth; it carries her into a new life.

In the same passage, Cisneros states the realities of domestic violence. Cleófilas, though seemingly isolated from the outside world, is all too much a part of the daily violence that men inflict on women. When she returns to Mexico, she may be escaping not only beatings and bruises, but death, hers and her children's, as well. She feels connected to the women in the news stories because her husband abuses her emotionally and physically. When he throws a book at her from across the room, she begins to realize that she can take the abuse no longer: "He had thrown a book. Hers. From across the room. A hot welt across the cheek. She could forgive that. But what stung more was the fact it was *her* book, a love story by Corín Tellado, what she loved most now that she lived in the U.S., without a television set, without the *telenovelas*" (52). The book is her property, her knowledge, her only form of power. Although she can own very little else in her relationship with her husband, she owns her knowledge and her fictional notions of romance. This shatters Cleófilas's last pretenses. Furthermore, it illustrates how her fantasies are also oppressive. Janice Radway believes that "the simple act of taking up a book addresses the personal costs hidden within the social role of wife and mother" and sees romance reading "as a form of individual resistance" (*Reading the Romance*, 12).

The implications of Cleófilas's husband throwing her book are many. The Corín Tellado romance in Latin America parallels the Harlequin romance in the United States. Such popular narratives prescribe for women how to be "good," and they reveal the consequences when one does not follow the script. As Jean Franco observes: "In the romance, the prime element is woman's adaptability to rules that she has not made and over which she has no control."[15] Often, the script may be predicted; the female protagonist will be seduced, repressed, and will ultimately sacrifice her intelligence. No matter how modern the society that the romance attempts to portray, the notions of the feminine are usually archaic.

Yet, what may seem archaic in Cisneros's narrative is a prevalent issue that many still face, that is, domestic violence and emotional abuse. Cleófilas wants desperately to hold onto her idea of romantic love, to be safe—at least in her mind. Just as a judge throws the book at a convicted criminal for punishment, Juan Pedro throws the book at Cleófilas. Her crime, in Juan Pedro's mind, may be that she can and does read, and that act gives her an independence which threatens him.

Ironically, however, this is the incident that leads Cleófilas to plan her escape. Once the repressive messages of the romance have ruptured, she can clearly see the violent situation she is in, and she "escapes the patriarchy which romances promise" (Radway, *Reading the Romance,* 12). In any case, Juan Pedro destroys any love or compassion that Cleófilas once held for him.

Pregnant with her second child, Cleófilas begs her husband for the money to go to the doctor to be sure that the baby is safe after her last beating. Afraid of being exposed, Juan Pedro at first refuses to allow her to seek medical attention. Convincing him to take her to the clinic becomes a transformative moment in Cleófilas's growth, for at the clinic she finds her means of escape. Juan Pedro still has economic control over her, an all-too-common reason that many women in Cleófilas's situation stay in abusive relationships. However, she saves money to take a bus back to Mexico. She may have kept the money that Juan Pedro gave her for the doctor's visit, or she may have used grocery money. So, unknowingly, Juan Pedro gives her a means of escape.

The conclusion of the story begins with a telephone conversation between Graciela, a clinic employee, and her friend Felice. Cleófilas relates her story to Graciela, and when Graciela sees the bruises that Juan Pedro has inflicted on her, she proceeds to ask Felice to help Cleófilas get out of her husband's home. Cleófilas is obviously grateful to these two women and is impressed by Felice, who has agreed to drive her to the border so she can return home to her father and brothers:

> Everything about this woman, this Felice, amazed Cleófilas. The fact that she drove a pickup. A pickup, mind you, but when Cleófilas asked if it was her husband's, she said she didn't have a husband. The pickup was hers. She herself had chosen it. She herself was paying for it.
>
> I used to have a Pontiac Sunbird. But those cars are for *viejas.* Pussy cars. Now this here is a *real* car. (55)

Felice uses the term "vieja" to symbolize something weak and frail. Although literally the word means "old woman," it is often used as Felice uses it—as a synonym for "pussy" or wimpy.

For Cleófilas, a woman who went directly from her father's home to her husband's without having a chance to command her own life, Felice is a shock. Felice avoids fixed gender roles, those which Cleófilas has embraced, if unwillingly, all of her life. As they drive across the creek, Felice lets out a holler, startling her two passengers as she says:

> *Pues,* look how cute. I scared you two, right? Sorry.
> Should've warned you. Every time I cross that bridge I do
> that. Because of the name, you know. Woman Hollering.
> *Pues,* I holler.
>     . . . That's why I like the name of that *arroyo.* Makes you
> want to holler like Tarzan, right? (55)

Felice, as the embodiment of Woman Hollering, has crossed the creek several times and assumes control. She hollers rather than wails, as the traditional Llorona does. Hollering implies strength and agency while wailing implies weakness, helplessness. Felice and the creek save people by finding them a refuge; La Llorona drowned her children in a moment of uncontrolled emotion.

Another way that Felice symbolizes power is through the holler as she crosses the creek, reminiscent of El Grito de Dolores, the Mexican shout of independence. El Grito holds great significance for Felice as a reminder of her personal independence and her revolutionary spirit.[16] Felice equates her holler with that of Tarzan, a gendered figure in English literature.[17] Felice is gendered as a butch lesbian, and Tarzan signifies her character.[18] In this description of Felice's holler, the author blends the Mexican legend of La Llorona with the fictional hero Tarzan. Both of these figures carry an ambiguous power. Tarzan is the son of a British nobleman, deserted in the African jungle as a child and raised by apes. He becomes lord of the animal kingdom, but when he returns as an adult to human civilization, he has difficulty adapting to humans after living with animals. He has power among animals, but among his own species he is seen as a misanthrope.

La Llorona, in the traditional narrative, is ostracized also. She is seen as a woman without control who commits infanticide. Both Tarzan and La Llorona are ambiguous in their characterization. Tarzan has royal power, but not among his own species. La Llorona seizes power over her children as she commits infanticide and takes control of her life. For lesbians, Tarzan symbolizes escape and freedom. Also, he always gets the girl, Jane. Cleófilas, by desiring Felice, desires her personal liberation. And by leaving her husband, Cleófilas straddles the border as Tarzan and Felice do.

This story consciously refers to the mythology of the border. The narrative begins when Cleófilas is taken across the border as the property of her husband. Her father "gave her" to Juan Pedro. The narrative ends with her return to Mexico, her home across the border, to her family of origin and to escape her husband's abuse.

In *Borderlands/La Frontera*, Gloria Anzaldúa discusses this mythology. Beginning with her own family history, in South Texas, she refers to the history of U.S. colonization in Mexico and the internal colonization of U.S. citizens: "The border fence that divides the Mexican people was born on February 2, 1848 with the signing of the Treaty of Guadalupe-Hidalgo. It left 100,000 Mexican citizens on this side, annexed by conquest along with the lands. The land established by the treaty as belonging to Mexicans was soon swindled away from its owners. The treaty was never honored and restitution, to this day, has never been made" (7). In the minds of many Mexicans on either side, the geographical border does not exist. Anzaldúa describes Mexicans who come to the U.S. as "economic refugees" (11).

Anzaldúa also describes the drastic circumstances that the economic colonization of many U.S. companies force on Mexicans: "For many mexicanos del otro lado, the choice is to stay in Mexico and starve or move north and live" (10). Although their economic situation may improve once they move to the United States, these displaced people most often live a dangerous day-to-day existence in a place that nurtures anti-immigrant sentiment. By situating "Woman Hollering Creek" on the border, Cisneros criticizes immigration issues, particularly the helplessness that immigrant women face. Cleófilas is from Mexico, and Juan Pedro is from Seguin, where he takes his bride to live. As a newlywed coming to a new country and new town, Cleófilas is dependent on her husband, especially economically. Yet, like many women, she faces the worst danger not from the outside world but from the internal world created by him.

Finally, two strangers are willing to help her escape her husband's physical and psychological abuse. Felice acts as the *coyote* for Cleófilas,[19] but instead of smuggling her to the United States from Mexico, she drives her to the bus depot so that she can return to Mexico—demonstrating the fluidity of the border.

With the help of these two strangers, Cleófilas escapes her abusive husband and unfulfilled *telenovela* life. She returns to her father and brothers' home in Mexico because she remembers the words of her father when she first left his home to be married: "I am your father, I will never abandon you" (43). On returning, Cleófilas enters an ambiguous situation. The reader would like to believe that she will see an end to her oppression, but it is evident that she will return to "the chores that never ended, six good-for-nothing brothers, and one old man's complaints" (43), another form of patriarchy.

Her willingness to leave an abusive environment to return to a town where she may be ostracized for her abandonment of her husband reveals Cleófilas's strength. She will cross the border, but, by virtue of her new personal liberation and development, she will probably resist the patriarchy and boundaries placed on her by her community. She imagines telling her family about this woman Felice who yells like crazy. By relating the story of Felice, an independent woman, Cleófilas becomes like the author, Cisneros, as she re-visions traditional myths and concepts of woman:

> Felice was like no woman she'd ever met. Can you imagine, when we crossed the *arroyo* she just started yelling like a crazy, she would say later to her father and brothers. Just like that. Who would've thought?

Who would've? Pain or rage, perhaps, but not a hoot like the one Felice had just let go. Makes you want to holler like Tarzan, Felice had said.

Then Felice began laughing again, but it wasn't Felice laughing. It was gurgling out of her own throat, a long ribbon of laughter, like water. (56)

Cleófilas, once unaware that independent women like Felice existed, finally has a positive role model. She admires Felice and will now tell her story, one which can be every woman's story. This "gurgling out of her own throat" is a reminder both of the way Cleófilas has internalized the creek and of her own shout of independence, or *grito*.

However, the reader is still offered an ambiguous ending. Cisneros purposely plays with ambiguity to enhance the narrative. She seduces us with her story as La Llorona seduces us with her wailing or hollering. Through the positive transformation of La Llorona, Cisneros rewrites history; she rewrites a legend that previously served to keep women in a subordinate position. La Malinche has been used as the symbol of the conquest and has been blamed for the conquest, a traitor to her race. La Llorona, as explicated above, has been represented as the weak, weeping woman. With the rereading of these and other female cultural symbols, women are given a significant role and positive attributes. Cisneros examines her own culture's treatment of women and gives women new voices and new ways to resist the patriarchy. Like La Malinche and La Virgen de Guadalupe, La Llorona has been evolving into a positive cultural symbol as Chicanas continue to write themselves and represent their own version of their history, as they continue to re-vision theory. The new Llorona, whom Cisneros portrays, no longer wails; she hollers. She is a *gritona*, demanding to be recognized as a strong, resistant figure who commands her own life. [20]

Through the rewriting of traditional cultural symbols like La Llorona, Cisneros articulates her political and theoretical agendas. In a *New York Times* interview, she emphasizes the importance of being an agent of change through literature: "I don't have to dream anymore about how to give insulin shots or how to give out condoms from planes. I can do my terrorist activities now by staying home and writing. I have the power to make people think in a different way. It's a different way of defining power" (Tabor, "At the Library with Sandra Cisneros," B2). Through her writing, Cisneros believes, she can be as effective as a *soldadera* in battle. Her battle is not a physical one, but a fight in which she struggles to create social change with her writing and imagination. A fiction writer has the power to make people think differently, to offer them options, even if those options are fictional characters and places that may be completely foreign. If a writer challenges the status quo in any way, readers will respond by resisting the new way of thinking, by considering the possibility of changing their view, or by adopting the author's view. The word, in the hands of a gifted writer, can be a powerful weapon and often can lead to political awakening. Indeed, poetry has been an influential weapon in the hands of revolutionaries throughout history.

Nations and their citizens are invested in their cultural symbols, especially those symbols that maintain the current power structures. The cultural symbols and mythologies that I am discussing in the context of the work of Chicana writers have been revised and reworked for centuries. These mythologies have become an integral part of society's collective consciousness. Cisneros states that she does not want to lose or abuse the power that she is given through writing, but that she wants to help her community. Maintaining this libratory consciousness makes her the interpreter of events that Anzaldúa proposes in her definition of theory. When Cisneros uses fictional characters to write about women's oppression, she creates the theories that women need to change their lives but leaves it to her readers to *agarrar la onda* (read between the lines) to achieve self-liberation.

Chicana literature, like Mexicana literature, is not always given the serious scholarly attention it deserves. Since the 1960s, however, Latin American literature has gained wide attention due to the increase in translated texts. Nevertheless, few critical studies have focused specifically on women's contributions to the field, and the texts that have been translated are often by male authors.

In the 1980s in Mexico, women produced and published such an impressive body of work (in quantity and quality) that the period has been referred to as the literary boom.[1] Consequently, Mexicana literature is now being considered more broadly for critique. With the exception of the proceedings of the conferences sponsored by the Colegio de México in which Chicana and Mexicana writers and critics meet annually, comparative critical studies of these two national literatures are scarce. Furthermore, many of the existing analyses are testimony to the patriarchal stranglehold on the publishing industry in Mexico. These critiques are indicative of the questioning of the legitimacy of women's experience as a subject for literature.[2]

Roselyn Constantino reminds us of the basic argument which still dominates much of the discussion around women's literature in Mexico: "According to many Mexican writers and critics, literature with explicitly 'women' themes, written from traditionally feminine spaces (like the kitchen in *Like Water for Chocolate* by Esquivel) or that explores women's desires to come into a style or a language of their own is still not seen as constituting 'good' literature" ("Resistant Creativity," 9).

Though the scholarly studies are lacking, there is a tradition of women writers across the Americas who have examined the value of looking at the feminine sites of creativity. Alice Walker explains how black women in the United States, as women who were not allowed (at certain historical times, by law), to express their imagination, had to find alternate means of artistic expression. One of these sites, as discussed by Walker, is the garden as the woman's domain.[3]

Although there is a large body of literature and scholarly interest is increasing, the biases still exist. These biases affect both the reading public and the writers themselves. Because of the general impression of women's writing, particularly feminist writing, many Mexicana writers do not refer to their work as feminist-based, although often the writing is women-centered and critical of capitalist patriarchy.

Though the stakes are high for Chicana writers who bring feminist issues to the forefront, the stakes are higher for Mexicana writers. Elena Poniatowska states in "Puentes de ida y vuelta" that Chicana writers are much more liberated in their writing than are Mexicana writers, a position most evident when the issues are sexuality or lesbianism. Yet, while it may seem to contemporary Mexicanas that the United States is indeed more liberatory vis-à-vis gay/lesbian writing, in fact, gay/lesbian censorship is equally strong in both countries. It just takes different forms.

### CARMEN BOULLOSA AND "LA NIÑA SALVAJA"

Regardless of the high stakes, many Mexicana writers are brave enough to challenge the patriarchy. Carmen Boullosa is one of those authors. She prefers that her work not be categorized as "women's writing," yet it is among the most daring and innovative of Mexicana literature today. While Boullosa may resist her works being labeled, her titles suggest feminist concerns, specifically, a political agenda.[4]

Boullosa, unlike Sandra Cisneros and Helena María Viramontes, does not ground her literary creation in existing cultural symbols; she has created a new symbol, La Salvaja, a model of resistance for women. Like La Llorona, La Salvaja comes out at night, and like La Gritona, she breaks away from stereotypes of femininity. The characterization of La Salvaja is reminiscent of Cisneros's "Loose Woman."[5] La Salvaja is the "bad girl" and the *mujer andariega* of *My Wicked, Wicked Ways*.[6] Like Gloria Anzaldúa's "nueva mestiza" (in *Borderlands/La Frontera*), La Salvaja is more comfortable with new affiliations.

Although Boullosa's work is women-centered, male characters figure in it as foils whose presence allows criticism of patriarchy. It is still common to see Mexicanas putting men at the center of their narratives, if only to make their work more widely accepted. Boullosa, however, does not present male protagonists simply to make it appear to her reading public that her work is legitimate. Her poetry, prose, and drama clearly demonstrate her rejection of patriarchal structures.

Because very little of Boullosa's early work has been translated into English, she is not widely known in the United States.[7] Because of the biases against women's literature discussed earlier in this chapter, her early work also has not been widely critiqued in her native Mexico.[8] One of the few analyses of her work is a chapter in Roselyn Constantino's dissertation, "Resistant Creativity." Constantino's analysis refers often to the violence in Boullosa's narrative, but it does not focus on her creation of a literary symbol which does everything possible to escape and reject that violence. This important new cultural symbol, which Boullosa has named La Salvaja, is a symbol of resistance for all women. Of primary importance is Boullosa's invention of the term "la salvaja": she has feminized the term "el salvaje" and appropriated it. "El salvaje" translates to "savage" or "barbarian." The phrase "La salvaja" is prevalent throughout Boullosa's work, and in a book of poetry entitled *La salvaja* (1989; all quotations in the text are from this edition), she defines her literary creation:

> La salvaja es una niña, es una muchacha, es una mujer. No tiene familia, no tiene memoria, no tiene edad. La salvaja no forma parte de esta genealogía o de aquella historia. Su futuro, si existe, se conjuga en infinitivo. A La salvaja

no le corresponde identidad alguna ni sabe lo que es la fidelidad. Todo en ella se desborda. Si algo la sustenta es su egoísmo inocente, su fervor por la batalla, su sensualidad alegre. Sólo su propio deseo es capaz de agotarla, sólo su deseo la destroza y la reconstruye. La salvaja es un río y es luz, es azul y es transparente, está en constante movimiento para ser siempre la misma y se desplaza tan rápidamente que creemos está quieta. La salvaja rompe con todo porque es ingobernable. La salvaja, sobre todo, es feliz. Para ella felicidad y vida son una y la misma cosa. Y éstos son sus poemas. Por supuesto, los poemas de una salvaja no son piedras preciosas. Sus poemas son sencillamente piedras que ruedan por el fondo de un río de cauce siempre cambiante, son el murmullo de esas piedras trashumantes por su vereda de agua.

[The Wild One is a child, a young girl, a woman. She has no family, no memory, no age. The Wild One has no part in this genealogy, or in that story. Her future, to the extent to which it exists, is conjugated in the infinitive mode. She lacks any kind of identity and knows nothing of faithfulness. She is all excess. If anything sustains her it is her naïve selfishness, her eagerness for battle, her joyful sensuality. Only her own desire is capable of exhausting her, only her own desire destroys and rebuilds her. The Wild One is a river and she is light, she is blue and transparent; she is in constant motion always to remain herself, and she moves so fast that we think her still. The Wild One knows no boundaries because she cannot be tamed. Above all, the Wild One is happy. For her life and happiness are one and the same thing. And these are her poems. Needless to say, the poems of a wild one are not precious stones. They are simply river stones rolling at the bottom of an ever-changing riverbed, they are the whispers of those errant stones in their waterway.][9] (7)

The narrator in this collection of poems traverses a land of self-discovery. She questions her role as poet and as child and woman. Through the answers that emerge from her poetry, we observe her ultimate refusal to play to her scripted role. Much like the girls and women in Cisneros's *The House on Mango Street, Woman Hollering Creek,* and *Loose Woman,*[10] Boullosa's characters write a new script for themselves while recasting their identity and escaping to a world where they have control.

In another of Boullosa's works, *Antes,* a coming-of-age narrative, the protagonist states that she will do whatever she must to save herself. She is reminiscent of many Chicana protagonists who find a means of escaping abusive environments, including, often, poverty. Esperanza in *The House on Mango Street* wants to escape her neighborhood and accomplishes this by writing herself a new home and future. Likewise, Alma Villanueva's narrator in *Mother, May I?* escapes an abusive past by writing about her pain and birthing herself to a new existence.[11]

*La salvaja* is characteristic of much of Boullosa's work, and throughout this book of poetry she demonstrates the rebellion of La Salvaja. The themes in *La salvaja* include innocence, infancy, girlhood, eroticism, and poetry. Boullosa divides her text into seven sections: "El hilo olvido," "Ingobernable," "Poemas desde la infancia," "Abierta," "Lealtad," "La infiel," and "La salvaja." These sections may represent specific turning points in the protagonist's life, yet all of them return to the search for self. The title of the book, *La salvaja,* shouts the narrator's rebellion.

La Salvaja is an egoist, but this trait is not presented as negative, for Boullosa also describes her through nature, woman in her "pure" form. The feminine embodies elements of nature: earth, wind, fire, and water. Many images of nature appear as representations of freedom: birds, air, water.

While there are representations of liberation in *La salvaja,* there are also symbols of oppression; darkness and prison demonstrate social norms. The body is presented in a negative form and as impure. The challenge is to overcome oppression by focusing on the liberating aspects of womanhood. In this way, Boullosa celebrates woman and denounces patriarchy.

Through the search for self and the explanation of La Salvaja, Boullosa arrives at the larger theme of her writing. She defines her dual struggle: an engagement with words to express herself converges with an effort to find and liberate her woman-self through writing. The body also represents liberation as it becomes a site of pleasure and discovery.

In her poetry, Boullosa maps the difficult path of a woman's rebellion in La Salvaja's world and presents her in all her complexity—as child, adolescent, adult woman. On reaching maturity, La Salvaja escapes the guards that stand between her and her liberation. The poem that ends the text, "Salvaja," expresses this escape, an escape that is not a conclusion of La Salvaja's struggle but a clearer path on her journey toward self-liberation. This one poem synthesizes several of Boullosa's themes: the role of woman and poet; factors in woman's life that contribute to her role; and woman's desire to flee from prison, that is, patriarchal society.

Boullosa's free (liberated) verse is appropriate to the content. Repeated references to flight and movement reinforce this theme. The narrator of "Salvaja" speaks in the present tense. La Salvaja is fictional, but her struggle is not. Through Boullosa's powerful language, the victory of La Salvaja becomes the victory of the reader, as the latter realizes that she can also achieve liberation.

In earlier poems in the collection, Boullosa presents many images of day, but in "Salvaja," there are more images of night. "Salvaja" begins:

> En las noches camino, corro, vuelo,
> sin distinguir
> recorro la tierra
> (Nights I walk, run, fly
> without differentiating
> I travel the earth). (148)

The night liberates La Salvaja. She can discover all that the day does not offer her. She is very lonely in the night, and her only companion is nature. Like Cleófilas in "Woman Hollering Creek," who turns to the creek for friendship, La Salvaja turns to nature for peace.

Despite the fact that she has more liberty in the night, she also fears the solitude and her lack of knowledge of how to live in the world with the "civilized":

¿Cómo podría conocer formas humanas?
Abro los ojos:
huelo peligro:
¡me echo a correr!
[How to know human forms?
I open my eyes:
I smell danger:
I take off running!] (153)

No me enseñaron a leer personas en las formas,
Nadie educó mis ojos.
Mi padre
es la llama ardiendo en el seco rosal
la llama triste.
[I was not taught to discern humans in the shapes,
No one trained my eyes.
My father
is the burning flame in the shriveled rosebush
the sorrowful flame.] (149)

We see here a symbol of formal education. The patriarchal system, as represented by the narrator's father, is the system which is attempting to pacify her and make her submissive and subservient to all worldly creatures. Despite her lack of "culture," however, she understands the conspiracy and is determined to win the battle between herself and society. She has personal power and, because of this, the masculine world fears her. La Salvaja threatens patriarchy.

A constant metaphor in the poem is flight—La Salvaja's immense desire to metaphorically escape the destiny she faces as a woman and as a writer attempting to interpret the world:

Pongo el dedo en el mundo.
Aprieto fuertemente.
Vuelvo rompecabezas la unidad.

[I put my finger on the world.
I press hard.
I turn it all into a puzzle.] (150)

This passage presents her interaction with the world: her power at first does not appear to be enough to combat her enemies, but along her path, she discovers her strength:

Alas no tengo:
Sí la piel delgada y aire, aire, aire,
por mis venas aire vuela,
La que rasga el camino que recorre
podría volar.
Pasos, pasos que tan bien rompen
¡sujétenme!
[Wings I lack:
But my skin is thin and I have air, air, air
air flying through my veins,
She who tears up the road she travels
could fly.
Steps, steps that rip so well
hold me!] (151)

Although La Salvaja has the desire to fly, she is also a realist. She is conscious of the obstacles she faces in her flight. In the above passage, she expresses her belief that flight is her right, but there are obstacles: societal rules and the obligations imposed on her as a female. La Salvaja is constantly aware of the forces working against her. Throughout the poem, she describes herself as an animal:

[Corro, corro,
¡Pongo y quito los pies
en la tierra arisca!
[I run, run
My feet touch and lift off
the surly earth!] (151)

Masco furiosamente
[I chew furiously] (152)

huelo peligro:
¡me echo a correr!
[I smell danger:
I take off running!] (153)

la rota bestia
[the broken beast] (155)

She runs when she encounters humans, she has the sensory powers of animals, and she intuitively relates to nature. For La Salvaja, the world is nature, and she cannot or will not relate to the material world. Nobody understands her, and at times she cannot even recognize herself:

Pies tengo
Alas no
¿Un rabo cuelga?
Tal vez adentro: es mi tórax hueco.
[Feet I do have
But not wings
A tail hangs?
Perhaps inside: my chest is hollow.] (151)

Here again, she is comparing herself with an animal; she is discovering her own form. What she is coming to realize is that the beast and the human have combined to fashion La Salvaja.

The woman in her is La Salvaja. She takes flight despite the forces ranged against her. She will write and begin the journey to discover herself more completely, but the journey will not end, because her struggle will continue as long as society fears her kind. The final lines of the poem reflect this struggle: "Los guardias no permitan que escapen, no dejen que esas fieras . . ." [The guards do not allow them to escape, do not allow those beasts . . .] (156).

Now that La Salvaja is freer because she has realized that her unique form is her power, she is more of a threat than ever. Society will see her differently and will not understand her; the person who knows herself is a threat to those who do not know themselves. Through her writing and through her power as a woman, which she now recognizes, La Salvaja has discovered her personal liberation:

> Cuando escribo esto es porque
> la rota bestia
> La salvaja que soy
> yo
> por los aires
> me he ido
> [When I write this it is because
> the broken beast
> The Wild One that I am
> me
> through the air
> I am gone] (155)

She writes because the Wild One in her has taken flight, leaving her calm so she is able to write.

In this final section, Boullosa describes a creature breaking out of confinement—out of the zoo for La Salvaja, out of the patriarchal structure for the writer. La Salvaja takes flight with physical wings; the writer's metaphorical wings are her new vision and power.

La Salvaja only begins to be articulated in Boullosa's poetry, but her presence is felt in other works. In *Antes,* we find her in the form of a sassy teenage girl who admits that she will do whatever she must to save herself. We also find forms of La Salvaja in *Mejor desaparece,* in which Boullosa utilizes the theme of orphanhood. Here the author avoids using a traditional genre; the fragmented form that she adopts adds to the other peculiar aspects of the story. The narrative is written with a third-person omniscient narrator, the collective child protagonist. The reader discovers early in the story that the characters are orphans; the mother has died, and the father runs the household. He does not do a very effective job, although he reminds the reader throughout that he does the best that he can and provides the children with what he considers to be their basic needs. He tells his children:

—Huérfanos de madre, pero no es por mi culpa . . . y les cuido el pan que se llevan a la boca. No me preocupo por ustedes, porque cada día encuentro un método mejor para cuidar su salud y su crecimiento.

[You do not have a mother, but it is not my fault . . . and I provide the bread you eat. I do not worry about you, because each day I find a better way to take care of your health and your growth.] (17)

Yet, the children constantly rebel against him until the end of the text, when his power has almost completely diminished. It is obvious that he is not providing them with what they truly need.

The majority of characters in this work are women; all are named after flowers, making them appear to be soft, delicate creatures. Some of the characters are also independent, strong characters reminiscent of La Salvaja.

The memory of their mother haunts the children; her spirit watches over them because the father is cruel and overbearing. The narrative begins with an explanation that sets the father up as the domineering patriarch:

Entró corriendo a la casa, ruidoso, alborotado, a punto de estallar, y lo oímos y sentimos antes de que empezara a dar los gritos horrendos que todos conocimos tanto y que él jamás repetiría. Entró como un niño, salvaje, alterado, sin respetar lo que llamaríamos el sabio ritmo encerrado entre los muros.

[He ran into the house, noisy, excited, about to explode, and we heard him and felt his presence before he let out those awful cries that we all knew so well and that he would never repeat. He entered like a child, wild, upset, without any regard for what we came to call the wise rhythm contained within those walls.] (7)

The father is not the only one at fault for the lack of family order; many of the children are troublemakers. They play jokes on the servants whom the father hires to watch them and oftentimes run them out of the house.

The children are constantly searching for their mother or, rather, are searching for answers about her death. The story "Aclaración" describes their frustration:

Ya lo dije pero lo recalco: mamá murió. No puedo entender cómo ni cuándo, porque somos muchos a pesar de los desaparecidos, los muertos y los deformados. Por todos lados podrá usted encontrar a alguno con mi apellido y todos los que lo llevan, hasta la fecha, son hijos de mamá.

¿De qué murió? Nadie nos lo ha dicho. Sé que no en un parto. ¿De furia, al enterarse por coincidencia de lo que iba a ocurrirle a su camada? Dicen que tampoco. Lo que sé es que la naturaleza de su muerte es contagiosa porque nos ha arrebatado vida a todos y lo seguirá haciendo a través de los siglos. Para colmo eso; con su aparición, papá nos privó de la capacidad de disfrutar de lo poco que nos quedaba con cierto gusto.

Y el anónimo, el anónimo que llegó anoche: No tienen, no han tenido nunca. Nacieron de una hoja; su cuerpo es un vestigio; son ruinas de un pasado que nunca fue presente ni futuro. Nada lo desmentirá nunca.

[I already said it but I will emphasize it: Mama is dead. I do not understand how or when because there are many of us, despite the disappeared, the dead, and the deformed. In many places you will find people bearing my last name, and all of them, up to now, are Mama's children.

What did she die of? No one has told us, but I know it was not giving birth. Was it from rage when she found out what was going to happen to her brood? Not that either, they say. What I do know is that the cause of her death is contagious because it has torn away the life of many of us, and will continue to do so for centuries to come. And to top it all off, by showing up, Papa deprived us of the ability to enjoy, that certain delight in what little we had left.

And the anonymous note, the anonymous note that arrived last night: You do not have, have never had. You were all born of a leaf; your bodies are but traces, remains of a past that was never present or future. Nothing will ever prove that false.] (25)

The above story demonstrates the constant presence of the mother even though she is dead. Her spirit and the mystery of her death haunt the children. She seems to have had many children, more than those who are living in the home, so it could very well have been that she died giving birth, but she did not. The children carry the mother's and the father's name, yet, the father's name is not used. Moreover, the mother is more important as the one who bore them. The father is physically present, but he is not as significant as the mother, who exists only as a spirit.

The last section in this fragmented narrative, "No desaparece," demonstrates the mother's eloquent but raw manner of talking back to patriarchy. Although the central characters in this narrative are the children, this last vignette presents the father narrating his own tragic story. He arrives home from work to find that he cannot enter. He cannot find his house key, nor does the doorbell work. He first believes that nobody is home, but he sees his children and hears noise. He literally begins to shrink as the windows become too high for him to see through; he becomes the size of the petunias outside of his home. He realizes at the end of the narrative that it would be better to disappear than to be trapped running among the blades of grass.

The father in this story loses all importance; the children cannot see him as he peers through the windows trying to get someone's attention. His significance diminishes as his image shrinks (read: as his phallus shrinks), suggesting the decreasing importance of the patriarch. Nobody can hear him insist that they open the door and let him in. Although he shrinks, he never disappears completely but is left to wander in the grass, which suggests to the reader that the horrors of patriarchy linger even when the physical "father" diminishes.[12]

## REPRESSION AND RESISTANCE IN COMO AGUA PARA CHOCOLATE (LIKE WATER FOR CHOCOLATE)

The works of Laura Esquivel and Carmen Boullosa are stylistically dissimilar and have been recognized in very different ways by the reading public. Laura Esquivel's *Como agua para chocolate* (*Like Water for Chocolate*) was an overnight success and was translated into several languages. A film version of the novel was overwhelmingly successful as well.

The form of the novel has been the main focus of critics.[13] Like Boullosa, Esquivel rewrites the role of women. However, Esquivel is less radical in representing the resistance of her women characters. Her feminism is not a radical feminism but a cultural feminism that parodies traditional models for women.

At first glance, *Like Water for Chocolate*[14] appears to perpetuate stereotypes of women and Mexico. Its positive reception in the United States could reflect an acceptance based on the inclusion of stereotypes that confirm certain biases: the hot-blooded Latin lover; the domestic Mexican woman; the obedient indigenous servant; the wicked mother; the jealous macho male; the impassioned mulatta; the Mexican revolutionary; and the white rapist settlers. On further consideration, however, it is evident that Esquivel is also parodying the stereotypes she presents. The wicked mother becomes the representation of patriarchy. Tita's lover, who marries her sister, instead of being the strong-willed macho who will rescue her from her fate to never marry and bear children, is weak and indecisive. The indigenous servant, Nacha, although she dies early in the novel, possesses celebrated supernatural powers.

Because of the historical period in which the novel takes place, *Like Water for Chocolate* is a literal border narrative. It also crosses borders through its form, one that has traditionally been associated with women—the recipe book. Esquivel wanted to legitimize her narrative by making it into a more traditional and male-associated genre—the novel.

While Esquivel's novel is one of the first in this format to make the best-seller list on both sides of the border, there is a history of this tradition starting with Sor Juana to Rosario Castellanos to Helena María Viramontes. Referring to American ethnic literatures generally and Latina writers specifically, Jacqueline Zeff states: "Food—its preparation, consumption, sensuality, and power—carries more than the memory of home; food is not only the message but the medium of love, the spirit, survival, even art itself."[15]

For some Chicanas, that memory of home is Mexico. In *Like Water for Chocolate,* the narrator is a Chicana who relates the story of her family through a series of "recipes, romances and home remedies." She is the grandniece of the protagonist of the novel, Tita de la Garza. Esquivel has made the kitchen the liberating space of women—but only for Nacha and Tita. Tita's two sisters have no knowledge of cooking; only through Nacha and Tita are recipes passed on and the culinary aspect of family tradition celebrated and maintained. Tey Diana Rebolledo, in *Women Singing in the Snow,* is referring to Esquivel's work when she states: "Chicano kitchens are filled with abuelitas, mothers, wives, and daughters mixing ingredients and making meals. Women are imaged as nourishers both physically and symbolically; therefore, it is only natural that Chicana writers have seized that nourishing space and have linked writing and cooking. Furthermore, there has been recognition recently that cooking is linked to women's way of knowing. This women's culture is just beginning to be seriously recognized as an intellectual tradition" (130). This Chicano tradition is the Mexican tradition in *Like Water for Chocolate* passed down through the generations to the narrator, whose national identity we do not discover until the end.

The focal character in my reading of this recipe book/novel is Tita, who becomes the main cook in her household when the servant Nacha dies. To be sure, Tita expresses her creativity in the kitchen. Not only is it the liberating space for her, but it is the world she understands best: "For Tita the job of living was wrapped up in the delights of food. It wasn't easy for a person whose knowledge of life was based on the kitchen to comprehend the outside world. That world was an endless expanse that began at the door between the kitchen and the rest of the house, whereas everything on the kitchen side of that door, on through the door leading to the patio and the kitchen and herb gardens was completely hers—it was Tita's realm" (7).

At the historical time of the novel, women had few options for creativity, at least few that were recognized as proper. Esquivel, through her characters, recognizes those limited options and celebrates them. The women of the middle-class de la Garza family are all groomed to be good wives and good daughters, which means that they study proper etiquette and learn to cook, clean, and sew. The one daughter who masters the art of cooking, ironically, is the one who will be unable to marry and have children. In her family's tradition, as the youngest, she will be responsible for taking care of Mama Elena until her death.

Although Tita becomes the family's main nurturer through the art of cooking, she is also the most-repressed family member. While she feeds her family both physically and spiritually, she deprives herself of love and nourishment, as many women still do. Society expects this sacrifice from women, though it does not see it as such but, rather, as the lot in life that the divine has chosen for women and that they must learn to accept without complaint. Tita begins to accept the repression, but she becomes strong enough to resist and end the cycle and break with tradition.

The opening chapter reveals that, even before Tita's birth, she was destined to live a life of sorrow:

> Tita was so sensitive to onions, any time they were being chopped, they say she would just cry and cry; when she was still in my great-grandmother's belly her sobs were so loud that even Nacha, the cook, who was half-deaf, could hear them easily. Once her wailing got so violent that it brought on an early labor . . .
>
> Tita had no need for the usual slap on the bottom, because she was already crying as she emerged; maybe that was because she knew then that it would be her lot in life to be denied marriage. (5–6)

This sensitivity to onions is passed on, but after two generations, the association with sorrow and sacrifice has faded. Tita's grandniece is able to liberate all of the characters by telling their story.

The opening of the narrative also makes it known that, "thanks to her unusual birth, Tita felt a deep love for the kitchen, where she spent most of her life from the day she was born" (6). Her love for the kitchen and her creativity give her mysterious powers. Since she is unable to marry Pedro, her sister Rosaura marries him—at the suggestion of Mama Elena. Pedro states that he is marrying Rosaura only to be close to Tita, since they will all live in the same house.

Tita uses her culinary powers to inspire emotions that help her resist accepting the union between her sister and Pedro. Her tears fall into the batter while she is making Rosaura and Pedro's wedding cake, and the wedding is ruined when all of the guests vomit after eating the cake.

Tita's culinary powers derive from years of apprenticeship with Nacha. Nacha and Tita make a strong connection from Tita's infancy. When Tita's father suffers a heart attack and dies, Mama Elena is unable to produce enough milk to feed the infant Tita. Nacha, never married or pregnant, is able to nurse Tita from her breast. When Tita is denied the opportunity to marry the man she loves, she is made to cook alongside Nacha. She learns Nacha's recipes and methods of cooking; she is also apprenticed to learn Nacha's supernatural powers.

In addition to recognizing women's ways of knowing in the kitchen, Esquivel presents their healing traditions. The carriers of the healing traditions in *Like Water for Chocolate* are Nacha and Morning Light. Morning Light is Dr. John Brown's Kickapoo grandmother, whose spirit visits Tita when she is staying with Dr. Brown.[16] Morning Light assists in Tita's healing with her teas and herbs as well as with her very presence. Dr. Brown and Tita never speak, but "from the first, they . . . established a communication that went far beyond words" (110).

Morning Light's presence and special healing powers remind Tita of Nacha. At the end of the novel, both Nacha's and Morning Light's powers assist Tita and Pedro in expressing their passion. Although ridiculed by those who reject nonwestern medicine, these two women continue to practice their healing traditions. They resist modern medicine's ways of healing and keep faith with the traditions of their people. Their therapeutic methods touch not only the body but also the spirit.

Throughout the novel, Mama Elena is determined to keep

Pedro and Tita apart, but while they are living in the same house, it becomes nearly impossible. Just as Nacha nursed Tita by some miracle of nature, Tita, despite her never having been pregnant, nurses her first nephew, Roberto, when Rosaura is unable.

Now closely bonded with her nephew, Tita is devastated when Mama Elena suggests that Rosaura's family move to the United States. She is more distraught when she receives the news that her nephew has died. For the first time, Tita talks back to her mother. When Mama Elena commands that Tita not cry over her nephew's death, Tita screams: "Here's what I do with your orders! I'm sick of them! I'm sick of obeying you!" (99). Tita blames her mother for Roberto's death because Mama Elena separated him from Tita, the only person who could feed him. She hides in the pigeon coop, shutting herself off from the world.

Unknowingly, Mama Elena gives Tita her freedom, although her intent is to send her daughter to a mental institution. Mama Elena calls Dr. John Brown and orders him to admit Tita. Dr. Brown, however, takes Tita to his home to care for her. For the first time in her life, Tita has nobody to look after and nobody from whom to take orders. John Brown shows her tenderness and teaches her about love. For several weeks, Tita does not speak a word. John Brown asks her to use phosphorescent chalk to write her explanation for not speaking. Her response is simple: "That night, when John Brown entered the laboratory, he was pleased to see the writing on the wall, in firm phosphorescent letters: 'Because I don't want to.' With those words Tita had taken her first step toward freedom" (118).

With the love that John Brown gives her, Tita discovers a new way of living: he helps her discover her voice. For the first time, she can be her own person; she can speak her mind without worrying about being punished. Just as there is power in words, there can also be power in silence when that silence is a choice.

Because life and cooking are one and the same for Tita, her depression causes her to lose her desire for cooking and eating. Katy, the cook in Dr. Brown's home, does not nurture Tita with the food to which she is accustomed. Only when Chencha (a de la Garza servant) brings oxtail soup to Tita does she finally speak and become animated once again.

When Tita returns home after her mother is crippled by men who raided her ranch, their relationship is different. Tita is no longer afraid of her mother. Moreover, their roles are reversed. Now that Tita is standing up to her, Mama Elena believes that Tita is attempting to poison her.

After Mama Elena dies, Tita moves back to the home where she grew up. Here, she is haunted by her mother's ghost. Not until she talks back to her mother's ghost does it stop haunting her. On one of the ghost's visits, it tries to condemn Tita for having sex with Pedro, and Tita responds angrily:

> I know who I am! A person who has a perfect right to live her life as she pleases. Once and for all, leave me alone; I won't put up with you! I hate you, I've always hated you!
>
> Tita had said the magic words that would make Mama Elena disappear forever. The imposing figure of her mother began to shrink until it became no more than a tiny light. As the ghost faded away, a sense of relief grew inside Tita's body. (199)

Her mother's condemnation does not diminish Tita's love for Pedro; in fact, her ability to finally go against her mother's wishes strengthens her love for him and for herself.

The final chapter jumps forward several years to the wedding of Esperanza, Rosaura's second child, and John Brown's son, Alex. Rosaura has since died, and Esperanza is free to break away from the oppressive tradition of her family. Esperanza and her new husband move to the United States because Alex has received a scholarship to work toward his doctorate at Harvard University. With nobody standing in their way, Pedro and Tita are at last able to be together freely.

Morning Light's theory is proven correct when Pedro and Tita are able to truly begin their life together. In John's laboratories, Tita had learned the lessons that his grandmother taught him about phosphorus: "As you see, within our bodies each of us has the elements needed to produce phosphorus.

And let me tell you something I've never told a soul. My grandmother had a very interesting theory; she said that each of us is born with a box of matches inside us but we can't strike them all by ourselves; just as in the experiment, we need oxygen and a candle to help" (115–116). The oxygen for Tita is Pedro, and because the couple has waited so many years to express their love for each other, their union is explosive:

> You must of course take care to light the matches one at a time. If a powerful emotion should ignite them all at once they would produce a splendor so dazzling that it would illuminate far beyond what we can normally see; and then a brilliant tunnel would appear before our eyes, revealing the path we forgot the moment we were born, and summoning us to regain the divine origin we had lost. The soul ever longs to return to the place from which it came, leaving the body lifeless. Ever since my grandmother died, I have been trying to demonstrate this theory scientifically. Perhaps someday I will succeed. What do you think? (116–117)

Tita and Pedro make love, and Pedro dies in ecstasy. Tita believes that without Pedro she will never again have her inner fire lit and chews on several matches to ignite herself and enter the luminous tunnel with Pedro, where they can live together forever in the "lost Eden" (245).

Under the layer of ashes created from their burned bodies and the remains of the ranch, a cookbook is discovered. It "tell[s] in each of its recipes this story of a love interred" (246). Tita's grandniece inherits the recipe book from her mother, Esperanza, and carries on the family tradition by following the recipes. Tita's refusal to let Esperanza accept the same fate as her gives future generations new options for creative expression.

Not unlike Cisneros, Esquivel gives her characters fresh ways of living that minimize oppression. At the same time, she celebrates women's "superior virtues and values."[17] Laura Esquivel enters the dialogue with Chicana feminists by redefining family institutions, critiquing patriarchy (as perpetuated by Mama Elena), and examining sexual identity and subjectivity.

*[I]t is third world women's oppositional political relation to sexist, racist, and imperialist structures that constitutes our potential commonality. Thus it is the common context of struggles against specific exploitative structures and systems that determines our potential political alliances.*

CHANDRA TALPADE MOHANTY

## CROSSING BORDERS

The fiction of Helena María Viramontes is involved in the unique praxis of third world feminisms as it simultaneously examines multiple issues.[1] As one of the most socially and politically conscious writers of today, Viramontes presents global concerns in her short stories and proposes international coalitions through her narratives. The short story "Cariboo Café" (in *Moths and Other Stories*) crosses borders literally, figuratively, and formally; it expands the borders of a Chicana/o world linking with other communities of the Americas.

The work of Chandra Talpade Mohanty helps to frame this discussion. In "Cartographies of Struggle," the introduction to *Third World Women and The Politics of Feminism*, Mohanty carefully avoids presenting her work as an overarching theory for third world feminist politics. She stresses throughout that her writing is an "attempt to formulate an initial and necessarily noncomprehensive response" to the questions she poses (3).

I cite the work of Mohanty because she asks important questions that lead to a critical dialogue about third world feminist politics. Mohanty continues with the following questions, critical for the ensuing discussion: "Which/whose history do we draw on to chart this map of third world women's engagement with feminism? How do questions of gender, race, and nation intersect in determining feminisms in the third world? . . . What are the methods used to locate and chart third world women's self and agency?" (*Third World Women,* 3).

The question of a foundational text or history of third world feminism is often debated. Eurocentric and Anglocentric scholars place their histories at the forefront of feminist thought. The project of many, then, has been to challenge that centricity and examine their own history of women's struggles for liberation in their respective countries and communities. Along with the examination of the intersections of gender, race, and nation, we must look at class and sexuality. These factors articulate third world feminisms because the method of third world feminisms is to confront many issues simultaneously.[2] For third world women, resistance is a daily practice, and that practice is living theory. That practice is not only theorized, but the materiality of oppression becomes the focus of the discourse.

Two of the sites which Mohanty names as being third world are Latin America and U.S. "minority" populations. Viramontes brings together these two sites by introducing Latino immigrants into her narratives. She presents not only the U.S./Mexico border, but also the contemporary situation of many Latino immigrant communities in the United States.

In California, the site of Viramontes's narratives, Proposition 187 passed overwhelmingly in 1994. It (had it not been overturned by the federal courts) would have disqualified any undocumented persons from public education, health care, and other social services.[3] This measure surely would not have "saved our state," as its proponents declared, by solving California's economic problems. It promised to turn children into informers against their parents. Doctors and educators would have been forced to report anyone suspected of being in the United States without legal documentation. All people of color, particularly Mexicans and Central Americans, as the targets of this proposition, would have been under suspicion. An accent, olive complexion, or Spanish surname would have been all one needed to become suspect automatically. It is ironic that people rally to deny basic human rights to the undocumented and yet are unaware of or in denial about how our government is largely responsible for creating the situation. Although the proposition was challenged before and after its passage, the conservative Right was anxious to propose such a law at the federal level, and it had widespread support.

Viramontes's work addresses these controversial political and social issues. While 187 was never enacted into law, its repercussions persist more than two decades later. With California's legacy of anti-Mexican sentiment, Proposition 187 did much damage by insinuating that immigrants should not be recipients of basic human rights.

Viramontes recognizes the experience with colonization and patriarchy that her characters share.[4] Mohanty claims that "it is the common context of struggle against specific exploitative structures and systems that determines [Viramontes's characters'] potential political alliances" (*Third World Women*, 7). In "The State, Citizenship, and Racial Formation," Mohanty emphasizes the importance of writing in these struggles when she states that "resistance is encoded in the practices of remembering, and of writing. Agency is thus figured in the minute, day-to-day practices and struggles of third world women" (*Third World Women*, 38).

Viramontes's reflections on writing support Mohanty's statement: "I myself invent time by first conjuring up the voices and spirits of the women living under brutal repressive regimes . . . [b]ecause I want to do justice to their voices. To tell these women, in my own gentle way, that I will fight for them, that they provide me with my own source of humanity" ("Nopalitos," 292). This excerpt expresses Viramontes's strong political commitment to writing and to women's lives and struggles.

She has assumed the role of scribe for her ancestors and other women who have fought and are fighting for social justice whether on a global scale or in their daily lives.[5]

The first published collection of Viramontes's work, *The Moths and Other Stories,* introduced a voice to Chicano audiences that would quickly become significant in their literary world and move into the mainstream.[6] Prior to *The Moths and Other Stories,* Viramontes had published in several journals and anthologies. *Under the Feet of Jesus,* her first novel, was released by Dutton in 1995. In that year, Viramontes was only the second Chicana to have published with a mainstream press (Sandra Cisneros was the first, with the publication of *Woman Hollering Creek and Other Stories* [1990] and the reprinting of *The House on Mango Street* by Random House [1988]).

The publishing industry is representative of the marginality of Chicanas and other women of color. One cannot help but question their motives when mainstream publishing houses take up the work of previously marginalized writers. Are they supporting the distribution of this literature to larger audiences because of the tremendous historical and cultural value that these writers offer, or are there underlying motives? To be sure, the issue is almost always a financial one. Publishing houses and other distributors of cultural production have realized that there is a market for Chicano and Latino literature. As important as it is that the literature be published and distributed, we must guard against its becoming exoticized as representative of all Chicano or Latino experience.

Viramonte's *The Moths and Other Stories* was printed by Arte Público Press, a well-regarded nonmainstream press, but her work is read and recognized by a diverse audience. Critics accept her work as the strong political message it is intended to be, and their unremitting interest has gained Viramontes the reputation she deserves. Seldom does Chicana literature gain the scholarly attention it merits prior to its acceptance into the mainstream. Large presses can afford sophisticated national marketing plans, while smaller presses often struggle simply to survive.

Few Chicana writers have been published by mainstream

presses because their work has not been seen as marketable and because of continuing overt racism and sexism. Furthermore, Chicana writers are sending political messages to the dominant community and to their own community by publishing with small presses. Many feel, however, that the move toward mainstream publishing is positive; the body of literature is growing, and interest in that literature is increasing. Yet, it is still rare to see Chicana literature that is not gender- or ethnicity-specific accepted by a mainstream press.[7]

Viramontes's work commands the attention of a broad audience because her subjects cross many boundaries. Although she presents women characters who resist and rebel, Yarbo-Bejarano states in the introduction to *The Moths and Other Stories* that she "does not present idealized versions of feminists successfully battling patriarchy. Acutely aware of women's dilemmas, Viramontes creates female characters who are a contradictory blend of strengths and weaknesses, struggling against lives of unfulfilled potential and restrictions forced upon them because of their sex" (8). Her characters face the decision of abortion in "The Long Reconciliation" and "Birthday." In "Moths," the protagonist comes of age as she faces her grandmother's death. "Neighbors" demonstrates the modern-day deterioration of a barrio community. The complete text of *The Moths and Other Stories* represents the modes of repression that Viramontes's women characters face and their means of resistance. Even in their simplest acts, we can see their rebellion.

Although her protagonists are mostly Chicanas and Latinas, Viramontes's audience is much broader. She presents it all: the inner-world influences of the Chicano community; the outer-world influences of the dominant Anglo community; and the influences of the many communities of the Americas. Through the telling of women's stories, she also reshapes the cultural perceptions of women and offers them new ways of living that minimize oppression. Synthesizing the projects of other third world women writers and forming bridges in the process, Viramontes critiques the many systems of oppression that her characters encounter.

Sonia Saldívar-Hull's concept of border, or "bridge," feminism informs Viramontes's "Cariboo Café." Saldívar-Hull affirms that Chicanas must call on their own unique histories and needs as women of color in order to explain their experiences and their various brands of feminism. While she recognizes that Chicana forms of feminism are receiving scholarly attention, what she proposes is a feminism specific to the literal and figurative borders encountered by Chicanas and other women who share similar bridge experiences. Saldívar-Hull not only addresses the border between the United States and Mexico, but also proposes a larger context in which to view feminist movements. She discusses women such as Domitila Barrios de Chungara from Bolivia, a miner's wife who sees herself in relation to socialist feminisms but articulates her allegiances in a way that makes it obvious that she loathes the bourgeois feminism to which she has been exposed. Saldívar-Hull recognizes that, if "compañeras like Barrios cannot allow themselves the luxury of bourgeois feminism, a possible alternative is this bridge feminism that deconstructs geopolitical boundaries" ("Feminism on the Border," 211). Saldívar-Hull locates Chicana agency within a larger struggle; she realizes that it cannot be isolated. Cherríe Moraga also makes this clear in the foreword to the second edition of *This Bridge Called My Back* when she states that a revised edition will "be much more international in perspective" (ii). This kind of criticism, one that adopts an international agenda, is most helpful for making the linkages between Chicana and Mexicana writers.

The main agenda in "Cariboo Café" is the deconstruction of geopolitical boundaries. No clear signifiers identify the nationality of the characters.[8] Only the ambiguous geographical border separates any of these characters from their homeland. The washerwoman, a central character who remains nameless throughout the narrative, becomes a universal character. When she tells her own story in the third section of the narrative, she refers to women searching for their missing children as "La Llorona."[9] Symbolically, she represents the many mothers of the Americas who have lost their children to war, gangs, or drugs. In the same way, the two child protagonists, Macky and Sonya, may be seen as children from any part of the Americas. Although they are warned about the police and immigration officials (La Migra, the Border Patrol), they could just as likely be citizens of the United States. Yet, the color of one's skin has long marked a person as displaced, foreign, or other—and, therefore, a probable non-citizen.

The Cariboo Café is represented as the home of "displaced people" who are in search of "a toilet of one's own": "They arrived in the secrecy of the night, as displaced people often do, stopping over for a week, a month, eventually staying a lifetime" (65). This passage synthesizes the migrant life of thousands of undocumented people. Many come looking for temporary work and, as the narrator notes, that search sometimes keeps them here indefinitely. Oftentimes, however, no matter how long they stay, they never lose their displaced status. The larger society will never see them as a part of their reality but always on the fringe of society, on the margins: "The plan was simple. Mother would work too until they saved enough to move into a finer future where the toilet was one's own and the children needn't be frightened. In the meantime, they played in the back allies, among the broken glass, wise to the ways of the streets" (61). The idea of a brighter future for these immigrants is having a "toilet of one's own." [10] Their needs appear simple; luxuries are not an option in their reality. Daily survival is the focus for the whole family and especially for the most innocent of all, the children.

The children's lives are influenced by the decisions of parents and grandparents. They quickly lose their innocence as they become indoctrinated into street life. The streets always represent danger for them: "Rule one: never talk to strangers, not even the neighbor who paced up and down the hallways talking to himself. Rule two: the police, or 'polie' as Sonya's popi pronounced the word, was La Migra in disguise and thus should always be avoided. Rule three: keep your key with you at all times—the four walls of the apartment were the only protection against the streets until Popi returned home" (61).

The children live in constant fear of strangers and the police. Most children fear strangers, but displaced children have greater reasons for fear—paramount among which is their fear that the police, who, as Popi suggests, are all La Migra "in disguise" (61).

Sonya and Macky's confusion begins after their return from the babysitter, when Sonya realizes her house key is missing: "Sonya considered her key a guardian saint and she wore it around her neck as such until this afternoon" (61). She lost it in the school playground when her classmate Lalo wrestled her to the ground in order to see her underwear. The loss of the key is symbolic of the loss of innocence for both Sonya and Macky. Because they cannot go home, they are exposed to the violence, oppression, and poverty in their neighborhood.

For Sonya, though, this loss is also a violation. The reader understands that she is already being sexualized in her pre-adolescence. After losing the key, she wonders how she will explain the loss to her family: "Sitting on the front steps of the apartment building, she considered how to explain the missing key without having to reveal what Lalo had seen, for she wasn't quite sure which offense carried the worse penalty" (61). Sonya is aware of the "penalty" for being a girl.

The narrator offers only these brief thoughts of Sonya's, but they are a revealing view of the church's influence on young girls. Rather than being concerned about the personal viola-tion, Sonya worries only that she may be found guilty of some sin. Because girls are socialized to believe that they are to blame whenever they are victims of any violation, Sonya imag-ines that she is at fault for Lalo's trying to see her underwear, as if somehow she provoked it.

Sonya's and Macky's confusion is a consequence of their position as latchkey children, a common phenomenon in con-temporary society. It is particularly common among the work-ing class and working poor, as both parents may have to work multiple jobs to meet the family's basic needs. Certainly, immi-grants compose a large percentage of the working poor. Leav-ing children home unattended may be dangerous, but many times there is no alternative.

Although other children might panic at losing their house key, Macky and Sonya, who have every reason to fear the police, are exposed to even greater danger. The four walls of their home are their only protection.

Sonya realizes they could wait at a neighbor's home until their parents return, but on their way there they witness an arrest, which sends them into a confused state. The children have been told by their father how they should respond if ever they see the police: "The polie is men in black who get kids and send them to Tijuana, says Popi. Whenever you see them, run, because they hate you, says Popi. She grabs Macky by his sleeve and they crawl under a table of bargain cassettes" (63). Popi has constructed a horrible image of the police for his children; ironically, he has done so to protect them. Other children are told to run *to* the police for protection, but displaced children are not protected by the power structure. "Hate" is not too strong a word for Popi to use in describing the feelings of the police toward illegal immigrants.

Macky and Sonya have lost their innocence early, for no child should be subjected to such destructive emotions. As their classmate Raoul's father is put into the police car, Sonya longs for her parents; Raoul's father represents all immigrants to her. The arrest frightens her. She imagines that this could happen to her family. Even after the police car leaves the scene, they run past moving cars and into dark alleys, worrying the whole time that the police might be following them. They are frightened by shadows that are "hovering like nightmares," probably their own nightmares of being taken themselves (64).

As if returning from a long journey, Sonya is relieved to see a place that might be a refuge for her and her little brother: "Across the tracks, in the distance, was a room with a yellow glow, like a beacon light at the end of a dark sea. . . . At least the shadows will be gone, she concluded, at the zero zero place" (64).

The second section of the narrative begins the story of a restaurant proprietor and cook who epitomizes the American way, the new world order. He describes his Cariboo Café: "I didn't give it the name. It was passed on. Didn't even know what it meant until I looked it up in some library dictionary. But I kinda liked the name. It's, well, romantic, almost like the name of a song, you know, so I kept it . . . But now if you take a look at the sign, the paint's peeled off 'cept for the two O's. The double zero cafe. Story of my life. But who cares, right? As long as everyone 'round the factories knows I run an honest business" (64). The owner/cook, although a working-class man, not a wealthy proprietor, begins his story by defending himself. He wants us to know his is an honest business and that he does not take advantage of his customers. The restaurant sign is a symbol, as he states, for his life. The name "was passed on," he mentions, as was his working-class status.

Yet, we find irony both in the name of the café and in this man's life. He believes himself to be better than his clientele, both in physical appearance and in social status. He describes his customers as "scum" (64). There is nothing romantic about the café or about his life. As long as the people who live "'round the factories" see him as honest, he doesn't worry. His words represent a philosophy that is particular to U.S. services and capitalism. About his restaurant, he states: "The place is clean. That's more than I can say for some people who walk through that door. And I offer the best prices on double burger deluxes this side of Main Street. Okay, so it's not pure beef. Big deal, most meat markets do the same. But I make no bones 'bout it. I tell them up front, 'yeah, it ain't dogmeat, but it ain't sirloin either.' Cause that's the sort of guy I am. Honest" (64). For this character, this type of honesty represents the "American way."[11]

The second-grade meat represents the ambiguity. Actually, his dishonesty makes sense to him because, in his eyes, he is serving only "out-of-luckers, weirdos, whores" anyway (64). Because his restaurant is in a neighborhood that he detests, he is a victim of the poverty of his class. To make himself feel that he is better than his clientele, however, he victimizes them by taking advantage of their undocumented status. The undocumented have no recourse if he abuses them.

Like his clientele, the restaurant owner is a displaced citizen, a misfit. He regrets not closing early on the day when all his trouble begins. The washerwoman "looks street" to him: "Round face, burnt toast color, black hair that hangs like straight ropes. Weirdo, I've had enough to last me a lifetime. . . . when I hear the lady saying something in Spanish. Right off I know she's illegal, which explains why she looks like a weirdo" (66). Immediately, he associates dark skin and speaking Spanish with breaking the law.

When some undocumented workers from a factory across the street are arrested, the washerwoman walks back into the restaurant. Just as he betrays the trust of the factory workers by snitching on them, he will betray her trust by turning her into the cops. He points to the place where the workers can be found; they have taken refuge in his bathroom, the same bathroom where another client, Paulie, overdosed. If the displaced are looking for "a toilet of one's own," the Cariboo Café is not the place to find it. Rather, it is a site of capture and/or death for society's displaced citizens. Instead of a refuge, the Cariboo Café is a wasteland for all who enter.

The wasteland is read as the "zero, zero place," the O's being the only letters lit on the sign. The sign has multiple interpretations, all pointing to the representation of these people's lives through the reflection of O. The double O may also be read as the number 8 (written sideways), or as a sign of infinite marginality. As displaced persons, the characters are viewed by others as infinitely marginal, if they are recognized at all. None of them can escape their poverty, but even if they could, their skin color and language would keep them at risk of becoming displaced even within the wasteland.[12]

The third section is where all the characters' stories intertwine to make up the larger narrative. This final section forms a critique of the capitalist values of the United States that threaten people like Sonya and Macky and the washerwoman by promoting war and poverty in their countries. The first two narratives set up the last scene, which begins as follows:

He's got lice. Probably from living in the detainers. Those are the rooms where they round up the children and make them work for their food. I saw them from the window.

Their eyes are cut glass, and no one looks for sympathy. They take turns, sorting out the arms from the legs, heads from the torsos. Is that one your mother? one guard asks, holding a mummified head with eyes shut tighter than coffins. But the children no longer cry. They just continue sorting as if they were salvaging cans from a heap of trash. They do this until time is up and they drift into a tunnel, back to the womb of sleep, while a new group comes in. It is all very organized. I bite my fist to keep from retching. Please God, please don't let Geraldo be there. (68)

Here the story of the washerwoman and her son is completed. Until this final section, the reader does not know why the woman imagines Macky to be her son. In this section, we learn that her son Geraldo has been kidnapped by the *contras* in her native country, and we infer from the above passage that the child was murdered and in the "heap of trash" with the rest of the missing children.[13] When she inquires about her son, the guard, who is not much older than Geraldo, says that he could have been involved with the *contras:* "Contras are tricksters. They exploit the ignorance of people like you. Perhaps they convinced your son to circulate pamphlets. You should be talking to them, not us" (68).

Again, Viramontes presents both the oppressed and the oppressors and demonstrates how all are victims in a country at war. The mothers of the missing children grieve and pray for their children's safe return. As in the case of the washerwoman, the situation is almost always hopeless: "The darkness becomes a serpent's tongue, swallowing us whole. It is the night of La Llorona. The women come up from the depths of sorrow to search for their children. I join them, frantic, desperate, and our eyes become scrutinizers, our bodies opiated with the scent of their smiles. Descending from door to door, the wind whips our faces. I hear the wailing of the women and know it to be my own. Geraldo is nowhere to be found" (69). Viramontes adapts a common theme in Chicana literature by giving La Llorona an international representation in "Cariboo Café," making her a more universal character. All of the women of the Americas search for their children in war-torn areas, whether in El Salvador or the streets of Los Angeles.

In the form of a prayer, the washerwoman pleads for the return of her son: "Today I felt like killing myself, Lord. But I am too much of a coward. I am a washerwoman, Lord. My mother was one, and hers too. We have lived as best we can, washing other people's laundry, rinsing off other people's dirt until our hands crust and chap. When my son wanted to hold my hand, I held soap instead. When he wanted to play, my feet were in pools of water. It takes such little courage, being a washerwoman. Give me strength, Lord" (70). The contradiction is that a great deal of courage and strength is needed to survive the poverty and oppression in her native country and her adopted country, the United States.[14]

Generations of women like her have done backbreaking work for the wealthy and their families while sacrificing the care of their own homes and families. The guilt of motherhood is strong here: what this mother feels is that her neglect of her son has possibly killed him. She pleads with the guard to give her information about Geraldo: "I promise, once I see him, I will hold him in my arms again, I will never, never scold him for wanting more than I can give" (70). The guard dismisses her by saying: "Don't be foolish, woman. Now off with your nonsense. We will try to locate your Pedro" (71). Geraldo becomes the representative of all displaced and kidnapped children. The guard does not see him as an individual; the children's lives do not matter, for these children are only more victims of war.

The washerwoman's words constitute another sad commentary on motherhood and the guilt that a parent feels when unable to provide for her children in what she considers an appropriate way. Viramontes never mentions another parent to share the child-rearing responsibilities. The reader can only assume that, in this war-torn country, the father is disappeared or dead.

The washerwoman, in a state of post-traumatic stress, imagines Macky to be her son as Sonya and Macky walk around confused, also lost. When she begins to doubt that Macky is her son, the washerwoman asks: "Why would God play such a cruel joke, if he isn't my son? . . . My heart pounds in my head like a sledge hammer against the asphalt. What if it isn't Geraldo? What if he is still in the detainer waiting for me? A million questions, one answer: Yes. Geraldo, yes. I want to touch his hand first, have it disappear in my own because it is so small. His eyes look at me in total bewilderment. I grab him because the earth is crumbling beneath us and I must save him. We both fall to the ground" (72).

The disappeared child is all too typical of the horrors of a country at war. Although Geraldo was in his own country, he was still a displaced person, if only because he was a child. And he violated the first two rules of displaced people that the narrator sets up. As a naïve child, he probably spoke to his kidnappers when they tricked him into believing they were his friends. Macky's father's advice to beware of the "polie" could have saved Geraldo's life. Geraldo, his mother says sadly, went to the store for a mango and never came back. She blames her own selfishness for his disappearance. The mango, in this story, becomes the symbol not of cultural survival or exotic richness, as in some narratives, but of disenfranchisement. Not only is Geraldo kidnapped, but, as his mother infers, he is killed and his body mutilated along with those of several other children. Those who are not murdered by *contra* forces are at the mercy of their repressive governments, without food, shelter, or compassion, and die a slow death. The only way to escape oppression involves incredible struggle, and few ever make it.

Geraldo's story becomes the story of all lost children. The washerwoman, convinced that Macky is Geraldo, chases him and grabs him so that she can protect him. She is the urban Llorona wandering the city streets in search of her son. She declares: "It is like birthing you again, mi'jo. My baby" (72). When she takes the children into the café a second time, the cook/owner betrays her and calls the police. In all the commotion, she will not let anybody take her Geraldo again and pulls Macky close to her. When the police arrive, she throws hot coffee at them: "[A]nd she begins screaming all over again, screaming so that the walls shake, screaming enough for all the women of murdered children, screaming, pleading for help from the people outside, and she pushes an open hand against an officer's nose, because no one will stop them and he pushes the gun barrel to her face" (74). Again, as a representation of the mothers of all missing children and as a universal Llorona figure, she screams out with grief to a crowd of spectators, "pleading for help" (74). The shoving of the gun barrel in her face demonstrates the nature of police force against the powerless. The gun becomes a symbolic penis shoved in her face that could kill her. Viramontes describes their pose as "guns taut and cold like steel erections" (74), a typical phallocentric image of war—a portrayal of the sometimes violent nature of masculine culture.

In countries and communities at war, this image would inspire fear, but the washerwoman calls on the strength of other women and even of her dead son to resist the police. In Viramontes's narrative, the stereotypical weak and powerless working-class woman becomes a warrior. Not afraid to fight back, she sacrifices her own life. If "resistance is encoded in the practices of remembering," as Mohanty states, the washerwoman is resistant throughout the narrative (38). Her nostalgia for her homeland and for her son gives her strength to fight against the forces that wish her dead. She is referring to the police officer when she says:

And I laugh at his ignorance. How stupid of him to think that I will let them take my Geraldo away, just because he waves that gun like a flag. Well, to hell with you, you pieces of shit, do you hear me? Stupid, cruel pigs. To hell with you all, because you can no longer frighten me. I will fight you for my son until I have no hands left to hold a knife. I will fight you all because you're all farted out of the Devil's ass, and you'll not take us with you. I am laughing, howling at their stupidity. Because they should know by now that I will never let my son go and then I hear something crunching like broken glass against my forehead and I am blinded by the liquid darkness. But I hold onto his hand. That I can feel, you see, I'll never let go. Because we are going home. My son and I. (75)

As she is shot and is "blinded by the liquid darkness," she imagines being with her son in death. The only thing "real" to her at this moment is her "son's" hand, and this is the image she takes with her to her grave. In death, she goes home. She dies defending the right to keep her son, to hold onto what she feels identifies her—motherhood.

The washerwoman's death represents both her salvation and her damnation. She, like many refugees, has searched for a safe place to live, a country without war. In her own country, she experienced war on a daily basis. Yet, once in the United States, she finds that war exists also in her refuge country, albeit in a different form. In the United States, she is the displaced person, the "illegal alien" that the government and many of its citizens use as a scapegoat to explain the grave problems that the country is facing. The U.S. government has created a situation that leads people to take refuge in this country by supporting repressive governments, and then it denounces these people, labeling them "aliens." In this way, the immigrants do not seem so much like "us," and imposing inhumane circumstances on them becomes easier.

Although "Cariboo Café" was written more than two decades ago, the same issues it addresses are still present. Helena María Viramontes reminds her readers of the importance of solidarity among third world women. Through the washerwoman's story, she tells the story of repression and the story of resistance of all third world women. If they form the international coalitions, which scholars like Chandra Mohanty and others propose, they can challenge the system of U.S. imperialism and patriarchy which creates and perpetuates the situations of war and poverty in the Americas.

## UNDER THE FEET OF JESUS

The first novel to record the struggle of the campesino through the eyes of a Chicano author and protagonist is Tomás Rivera's . . . Y no se lo tragó la tierra (1971). The author incorporates a collective protagonist to tell the story of the farmworker. Ramón Saldívar notes: "We see glimpses of a stark world of class and racial oppression: the death of a child, shot when he pauses from working to get a drink of water; a mother anxiously praying for her son who is away fighting in Korea; another child's first shocking encounter with adult sexuality; an agoraphobic woman painfully venturing out into the marketplace; a truckful of migrant farmworkers speeding northward in the night toward the agricultural fields of the Midwest" (*Chicano Narrative*, 79). Rivera's novel documents a story until then untold.

While "Cariboo Café" offers us a look into urban Los Angeles, Viramontes's first novel, *Under the Feet of Jesus,* gives the reader a look into California's rural San Joaquin Valley through the eyes of Estrella in a further depiction of the resistance that identifies the author's work. *Under The Feet of Jesus* adds yet another voice to the narratives about migrant workers and their lives. The story is told by a young Chicana giving voice to her and other women's experiences. Moreover, by dedicating her novel to César Chávez and to her parents, "who met in Buttonwillow picking cotton," Viramontes merges the personal with the political.

The protagonist is an adolescent girl chronicling the story of her family while making her own journey into womanhood. The novel, like other works in this study, examines the daily resistance of those who live under oppressive conditions. Estrella and her family, like many migrant families, guarantee themselves a secure future. The opening chapter reveals their dilemma: "The silence and the barn and the clouds meant many things. It was always a question of work, and work depended on the harvest, the car running, their health, the conditions of the road, how long the money held out, and the weather, which meant they could depend on nothing" (4). A missed day of work could mean that one or more family members would go to bed hungry.

Estrella, as the oldest child, takes on responsibilities which would have been her father's had he not abandoned the family. She acts as the second parent, a role that she takes very seriously. By being forced to take on this role, she crosses age and gender borders. She recalls working in the fields alongside her mother, Petra, since the age of four and her mother's being pregnant but hauling several pounds of cotton. As a single parent, Petra has no choice but to risk her and her unborn child's health. The children who are too young to work are rocked to sleep on the bags of cotton or tied to the mother's waist with a rope.

Estrella's lost innocence includes a constant fear of the Immigration and Naturalization Service. Walking home from the fields one day, she encounters La Migra: "She startled when the sheets of high-powered lights beamed on the playing field like headlights of cars, blinding her. The round, sharp white lights burned her eyes and she made a feeble attempt to shield them with an arm. The border patrol, she thought, and she tried to remember which side she was on and which side of the wire mesh she was safe in. The floodlights aimed at the phantoms in the field. Or were the lights directed at her? Could the spectators see her from where she stood? Where was home?" (60). As Estrella tries to block out La Migra's floodlights, she looks like a hunted animal trying to decide which side of the fence (border) is enemy territory, because in the United States there are no demilitarized zones. Trying to minimize the horror she feels, Estrella likens her encounter with La Migra to a game of baseball where the goal is to reach home.

This scene is reminiscent of "Cariboo Café" and those children's fear of La Migra. Macky and Sonya's father warns them to run and hide from the "polie," or La Migra. Petra, however, encourages Estrella to stand up and challenge them, although the challenge is without merit: "Don't run scared. You stay there and look them in the eye. Don't let them make you feel you did a crime for picking the vegetables they'll be eating for dinner. If they stop you, if they try to pull you into the green vans, you tell them the birth certificates are under the feet of Jesus, just tell them" (63).

Petra wishes that the government did not have this control over their lives. Realistically, La Migra should not be a threat to her children because they are U.S. citizens. However, the Border Patrol can prey on anyone it suspects of not being citizens.

Petra also realizes that those who feed this country are seen as criminals; in actuality, what is truly criminal is the substandard conditions in which farmworkers live. Though their work nurtures us in the most basic ways, they are often unable to properly feed, clothe, and educate their own families. In light of the developments of 9/11, this population is further threatened as it continues to struggle against poverty and for human rights.[15]

Estrella's mother, Petra, despite her limited resources, houses eight people in a one-room wood-frame bungalow. Only a thin blue sheet separates two sleeping spaces. Before Perfecto Flores comes into their lives, and after Estrella's father abandons them, Petra and her five children moved from home to home "to a cheaper rent they couldn't afford" (14). Though they live a life of poverty, family ties hold them together.

Although Petra wants to stay strong for her family, she cannot hide her greatest pain: the abandonment by her husband. She keeps a constant vigil for a husband who will never return. In reference to him, she thinks: "Was it he who had the nerve to disappear as if his life belonged to no one but him?" (17). As a mother, Petra's life is not her own. She will not abandon her children because she feels an obligation as a mother. She would not leave her husband because she feared he would become violent if she left. Her *comadres* warned her that he would stalk her if she left, because it would be "a slap in [the] face." She is trapped by the patriarchy and her fear of violence, so she remains and becomes the abandoned woman.

Alongside Estrella's and her family's story is the story of two cousins, Alejo and Gumecindo. They are also migrant workers, two young men from Texas. The cousins trespass in the peach orchards at night to pick fruit to sell at the flea market, which for them is a daily act of survival. As they are working, they have a clear view of Estrella and her family. One evening when Estrella is swimming in the canal, Alejo first notices her. He, under the pretense of offering the family a gift, arrives at Estrella's home with a sack of peaches and leaves more mesmerized than before: "Alejo did not really see Estrella's face, her pierced but bare earlobes which were long and oval. Did not see the deep pock scar above her eyebrow from a bout of measles or the way her eyes had green specks like her father's. What he saw was the woman who swam in the magnetic presence of the full moon, a woman named Star" (46).

Because of her abbreviated childhood and the nature of her life, Estrella does not have many opportunities to develop friendships. Yet, she does experience romantic love with Alejo. Though the two do not have sex, she experiences a symbolic sexual awakening and runs home to the barn to relive the moment in her mind: "She caught the flow of sun, felt the laser heat slowly penetrate her palms he had kissed, saw the blood of her body, a brilliant reddish pink rose, and she laughed" (90). The barn becomes a symbol of her sexual awakening: entering the barn was once forbidden her, but after her experience with Alejo, Estrella's interest is piqued.

While crossing the border between adolescence and womanhood, she also must cross the border between her traditional Mexican family's world and the Anglo world to which she is exposed when she steps out of the safety of her own family. In school, it is obvious to Estrella that the teachers treat the migrant children differently:

> She remembered how one teacher, Mrs. Horn, who had the face of a crumpled Kleenex and a nose like a hook—she did not imagine this—asked how come her mama never gave her a bath. Until then, it had never occurred to Estrella that she was dirty, that the wet towel wiped on her resistant face each morning, the vigorous brushing and tight braids her mother neatly weaved were not enough for Mrs. Horn. And for the first time, Estrella realized words could become as excruciating as rusted nails piercing the heels of her bare feet. (25)

The painful irony in this is that, within her limited resources, Petra's mother takes pride in properly caring for her children.

Estrella is disillusioned with the educational system and refuses to learn to read, although she understands the importance of language and words. Mrs. Horn's methods are demeaning, and Estrella does not see the usefulness in her lessons. Although the relationship between Estrella and Perfecto Flores is problematic, it is he who inspires her to learn how to read. She realizes how Perfecto's tools help him earn a living, and Estrella can connect with this. She sees meaning and usefulness in his methods. As he shows her ways of "building, rearranging and repairing" her life, she realizes the practical uses of learning to read and developing language. In assisting Perfecto Flores with his handiwork, she learns the tools' uses: "Tools to build, bury, tear down, rearrange and repair, a box of reasons his hands took pride in. She lifted the pry bar in her hand, felt the coolness of iron and power of function, weighed the significance it awarded her, and soon she came to understand how essential it was to know these things. That was when she began to read" (26). Estrella learns the positive power of words and tools. She also learns how both can be dangerous weapons.

Early on, Estrella also learns the injustices farmworkers face in the fields and the irony in the way that the fruit of their labor is marketed:

> Carrying the full basket to the paper was not like the picture on the red raisin boxes Estrella saw in the markets, not like the woman wearing a fluffy bonnet, holding out the grapes with her smiling, ruby lips, the sun a flat orange behind her. The sun was white and it made Estrella's eyes sting like an onion, and the baskets of grapes resisted her muscles, pulling their magnetic weights back to the earth. The woman with the red bonnet did not know this. Her knees did not sink in the hot white soil, and she did not know how to pour the baskets of grapes inside the frame gently and spread the bunches evenly on top of the newsprint paper. She did not remove the frames, straighten her creaking knees, the bend of her back, set down another sheet of newsprint paper, reset the frame, then return to the pisca again with the empty basket, row after row, sun after sun. The woman's bonnet would be as useless as Estrella's own straw hat under a white sun so mighty, it toasted the green grapes to black raisins. (49)

This is an important description of the contrast in the marketing of a product with the labor that goes into production. A
farmworker's labor is rarely recognized. Consumers walk into
supermarkets and see the neatly stacked produce; the marketing agencies "clean up" the image of families working in the
hot sun for low wages. Even in California, the setting of the
novel, where there exists a large agricultural industry, farmworkers are invisible to most. If their presence in the fields goes
unnoticed, then certainly their exploitation is rarely considered
by the general population.

Another factor that figures in their mistreatment is the lack
of proper medical care. This issue is explored through the
character of Alejo. He suffers from heat exhaustion, a common
health concern of farmworkers. Another mutual threat, pesti-
cide poisoning, is most likely an additional cause of his serious
illness. Alejo almost dies as Estrella's family seeks medical attention for him. He lives with Estrella and her family while he
is sick, with Petra only suspecting his and Estrella's bond.

At the clinic, they encounter familiar biases from the nurse.
The family has a total of $9.07, and the nurse wants to charge
them $10.00 for her services: "Petra was outraged—¡Diez
dólares! ¿Y por qué diez? No más para decir que está enfermo
el joven. Por gratis yo le digo la misma cosa. ¡Qué racketa!"
(144). Because the car needs gas in order for the family to take
Alejo to the hospital, they must keep the little money they have.
They do not want charity, Estrella thinks to herself; they only
need a way to stretch their resources.

As a traditional, even ancient, form of business, Perfecto
Flores wishes to barter his services for payment. The nurse,
who lives in a protected world nothing like the world of Estrella and her family, cannot see the urgency of their situation: limited resources and a dying friend. Petra and Estrella
resent the nurse's arrogance and unwillingness to barter. To
Petra, the nurse appears superficial, and she resents her for
this: "Even the many things on the nurse's desk implied fak-
ery; the pictures of her smiling boys (Who did they think they
were, smiling so boldly at the camera?), . . . a pile of manila
folder files stacked in a strange way that seemed cluttered and

disordered. She wore too much red lipstick, too much perfume and asked too many questions and seemed too clean, too white just like the imitation cotton. She may fool other people but certainly not her" (141).

Perfecto Flores hands the money to the nurse. But as they walk to the car, Estrella's anger heightens and she gets a crowbar out of the car to threaten the nurse and take back their money. When the nurse refuses to return the money, Estrella begins smashing the articles on her desk. Later, when Alejo asks Estrella if she hurt the nurse, she replies: "—They [dominant society] make you that way, she sighed with resignation. She tried to understand what happened herself. You talk and talk and talk to them and they ignore you. But pick up a crowbar and break the pictures of their children, and all of a sudden they listen real fast" (151).

In this scene, the crowbar, one of Perfecto's tools, becomes her literacy and way to take direct action. Mrs. Horn's methods of speaking do not serve her in this situation, although at first Estrella attempts to express her anger with words.

Perfecto drives to the hospital in Corazon, and the family drops Alejo off. Perfecto, trying to convince Estrella, says to her: "They'll take care of him, believe me" (155). We never hear of Alejo again, and we can only surmise his fate.

Although Alejo is not the center of Estrella's life, her symbolic sexual awakening with him allows her to gain other forms of liberation. In the barn, she notices the chain that opens the trapdoor and that has always been there but begins to question its purpose. As she pulls on the chain, it resists only slightly: "Estrella noticed her hands. Once filled with light, her palms were now tainted with brick red rust" (90). For once, she feels unafraid to enter the barn, and her curiosity about the chain will change her life. Her view of the world changes dramatically after she gains empowerment.

By the novel's end, Estrella has come full circle. While she stands on the barn's roof, she has a bird's-eye view of her world. She has found her voice of resistance. She has become a hope for future generations: "Estrella remained as immobile as an angel standing on the verge of faith. Like the chiming bells of the great cathedrals, she believed her heart powerful enough to summon home all those who strayed" (176). Estrella (Star) sees herself as a guiding light, like the North Star. She breaks the chain of the trapdoor that leads to the roof, finally overcoming her fears. It is at that point, on the roof of the barn, that she reaches maturity.

As a result of these experiences, Estrella's acts of daily resistance will continue to guide her life. Her struggles and actions will counter the expectations of mainstream society.

# AFTERWORD

Necesitamos teorías *that will rewrite history
using race, class, gender and ethnicity as categories of analysis, theories that cross borders, that
blur boundaries—new kinds of theories with new
theorizing methods.*

GLORIA ANZALDÚA

My project or "story" began in 1990 as a graduate student.
As a woman I wanted to tell the story of brave Chicanas and
Mexicanas who battled patriarchy. I hoped to describe the
challenges, the struggles, the successes and sometimes failures
of women who resist accepting the role that previous generations have handed down to them. I wanted to tell the story of
the brave women who write about once-forbidden subjects and
who have brought to life rich literary characters who question
traditional, narrow interpretations of womanhood.

While part of my early quest took place in Mexico City,
the latter part of my search took place in Málaga, Spain. The
beginning of the story stresses the importance of building support networks in the academy as a survival strategy; the continuing story emphasizes the same message. In the more than a
decade that has passed, I was hired to a tenure-track position
and earned tenure, promotion, and sabbatical. I learned a great
deal about myself through the experience of living abroad, and
the places that I lived—Mexico and Spain—connected me on
a personal level to my history.

As this project comes to a close, I have reflected on the development of this work and of myself as a scholar. My theory, my
modes of resistance, contained in the form of a book, are an ac-

cumulation of my own experience as a Chicana in a variety of international settings. By melding my story with the stories of the literary characters I have discussed here and their acts of resistance, the resistance has become the method. If theory is the lived experience, then the writers and the literary texts that I engage in these pages are aiding readers in their own processes of self-discovery and self-creation. This Afterword, then, braids these processes together with my own journey— all threads in the variegated and larger collective tapestry of women of color in the academy. In speaking out against silence and marginalization, our very existence and survival become a form of resistance.

## TEACHER

When people ask me what I do for a living, I respond: "I teach." The reality is, however, that as a tenured university professor, teaching is only one of several responsibilities, administrative and otherwise. Yet, of all that I do in my position, it is teaching that has always given me the most joy. In my naïve moments, I believe that all university professors do what they do because of the joy that teaching offers. What is it precisely about teaching that makes it a blissful experience? Part of the answer is that, as a teacher, I am also a student. Teaching is a natural career choice for a lover of learning. Yet, societal expectations of women of color would not place us in the role of university professor.

As a student, I felt liberated as I learned, through the various academic disciplines but mostly through literature, my major field of study, about worlds unfamiliar to me. Learning to think critically and to express myself through the written word was liberating. When I chose to pursue a PhD and a career in academia, my desire was and continues to be to assist students in their own liberation.

The classroom or community that I aim to create is certainly Freirian based. I was introduced to Paulo Freire in graduate school in a course on theories of teaching; since then, student-centered teaching is all I have ever practiced. Even in large lecture courses, I encourage dialogue and recognize student experience with course material as the point of reference for dialogue.[1]

Being a first-generation college student, I was not raised with a familiarity of the culture of the academy. In order to survive, first-generation college students are forced to learn how to function in this unknown culture. While I brought with me my own set of cultural values, those values seemed to contradict what I would have to learn: a set of unwritten rules. If one does not learn the rules of the academy, one becomes vulnerable to immobility and anonymity.

## SCHOLAR

After being introduced to Chicana literature as an undergraduate, I wanted to continue to read and critique more works by Chicanas; I wanted to be like a preacher, spreading the word of Chicana writers. Of the many literature courses I took as an undergraduate English major, the Chicana literature courses I took in the Chicano Studies Department nurtured me, because, while Chicana writers spoke to universal issues, they also spoke to my cultural experience as a woman and as a Chicana from a working-class background. That passion for literature is what led me to the world of academia, and that passion is what keeps me here.

Sadly, this transnational feminist work and the voices that speak of the experience are not highly valued across multiple disciplines. To read the rich literature produced by Chicana writers, students must take course work in ethnic studies departments or women's studies departments, since many "mainstream" departments do not value "oppositional voices."

As a discipline, Chicana/o studies has now produced many excellent critiques of the male-centered nationalism of the 1960s and the 1970s. Those who were often silenced during the Chicano nationalist movement, namely Chicana feminists and queer scholars, have voiced many of those critiques.[2] And yet, an uncritical male-centered nationalism is resurfacing in some settings. The expected culprits—the patriarchal *veteranos*—have retooled, adapted, and have been decent allies in some fights. It is often the younger male scholars who are less reliable as allies, although they supposedly "know better." Their liberation politics still excludes a critique of gender politics. Sadly, these potential allies are often more concerned with their own job security and personal prestige than with building coalitions across diverse communities. Equally disappointing are those who do not yet see the significance of including gender and sexuality as analytical categories in their own scholarship or in their teaching.[3]

There are many events that point to the biases within traditional departments and Chicano Studies departments. In 2000, a well-published Chicana professor-scholar-activist was denied tenure by her senior male colleagues in a California Chicana/o studies department. In 2002, at another California university, a Chicana was hired for her groundbreaking feminist activist scholarship but was undervalued (read: she was perceived as threatening) for doing her work. In 2004, another had to fight a tenure battle because her feminist scholarship was not seen as valid within her field. These women were attacked by the dominant culture of the university and by those within their more intimate scholarly circles.

Then there are those women who have found that the road to acceptance from those in positions of power is to adopt the male culture; they might have intellectual knowledge of feminism, but there is nothing in their behavior that represents sisterhood. One colleague recently told me that, before entering the academy, she believed it would be a utopia, an ideal society with a free exchange of ideas, a respect and appreciation for difference, and, foremost, a community of enlightened and progressive thinkers. After more than thirty years in the profession, she is still looking for that utopia. What has become evident is that patriarchy and hegemony also work through women and the liberal academy. There is no guaranteed safe space.

Fragility is present in our physical, psychological, and spiritual lives. Demoralization becomes an occupational hazard and is not easy to escape. Everyone in the academy is affected by its culture, and "marginalized" groups are affected in very particular ways. Women have distinct challenges as they function in the male-dominated culture of the academy. Women of color, even within their own departments, still sometimes face hostility when trying to place discussions of gender and sexuality at the forefront.

## TRANSNATIONAL FEMINIST MOVEMENTS: NORTH AND SOUTH

The intellectual field is not always a receptive one; transnational feminist scholarship is still a new phenomenon, although Chicana/o studies has always been a transnational endeavor. As I describe in the Preface, the idea to write about Chicana writers alongside Mexicana writers was born in Mexico while I was studying there. At that time, little work had been done on transnational feminist movements, particularly comparing feminisms spanning North and South. Traditional comparative literary studies have tended to focus primarily on comparisons of East and West. While more work along the North-South global axis has been attempted since the mid-1990s, there is still only a limited amount of such scholarship.

On beginning the project, I wanted to believe that there would be support from scholars in the fields of literature—Mexican and Chicana/o—and anyone interested in moving comparative studies in a North-South direction. Chicana and Chicano studies has always been transnational, after all. With its geopolitical connections to Mexico and Latin America, its comparative examination of historical as well as contemporary issues has been ongoing since the formal development of the discipline. Furthermore, there have been established programs in Chicano studies in Europe since the 1970s. The support that I anticipated for my transnational project from certain "experts" in the field, however, was not forthcoming.

Sometimes, it is our own who censor us. Gloria Anzaldúa has dubbed this phenomenon "homo-phobia"—fear of going home, or fear of our own most intimate circles. This homophobia acts as a disciplining of "unruly subjects."[4] I experienced this type of regulation from a former professor when he declared: "You cannot do that [a comparative project]; Mexicanas know nothing about Chicanas and Chicanas know nothing about Mexicanas." Aside from his attitude being purist, territorial, and a-historical, his lack of support for my work and for me, his former student, disturbed me. Another former professor was concerned that I was not receiving "proper guidance" because I had elected to conduct such a study.

From the "other side," a Mexican scholar whom I encountered at a national conference announced to me her irritation that I would even consider such a study. Just a few years later, this same person came out with a book of similar comparative work—which she had discredited only a few years before. A coincidence, perhaps. However, when I saw her again after her book was in print, she remembered me and the conversation went something like this:

> I: No sé si te acuerdas de mí. Nos conocimos . . . (here, she cut me off)
> SHE: Sí, y yo te dije que no vale la pena tu proyecto. Pues, así es. (She shrugged her shoulders.)

Because she recognized me immediately and remembered that she had told me that my proposed project did not make sense, I might have expected a different response from "Well, that's the way it goes."

Much could be read into that brief conversation. Initially, I interpreted it two ways: maybe, when I first met her, she had already begun working on her book project and did not want someone else to beat her to the punch; or she really did think the project unworthy at the time, but after our discussion, perhaps she began to rethink it. Either of these possibilities would be understandable to me. It was her self-righteousness at our second meeting that was problematic. She was a senior professor at a private Mexican university; I was a doctoral candidate. Had her attitude been different, I would have congratulated her on her work, told her that I was pleased that she was making this contribution to the field, and perhaps suggested that we work together on future projects. But instead I walked away wondering what kind of world I was entering where those who might be my allies could treat me so haughtily.

Still a student, I was in a vulnerable position, questioning my work and struggling to write. To balance the questionable motives of this scholar and others, I had a strong support network and mentors who offered support and "proper guidance." Reflecting on that experience in Mexico City after more than a decade, reminds me of the fragility one faces in academia.

## TRAVELER

My academic journey has been that of an envoy, a traveler. My fourteen months in Mexico in the early 1990s, while helping to inform my scholarship, also gave me the unexpected experience of a sense of belonging. While my dress and even my demeanor might have given me away as an *estadounidense,* I felt a sense of citizenship that I do not experience in the United States, where I was born and raised and where my family has been for generations. I did not stand out physically in Mexico. And even when people I met learned that I was from the United States, they were either knowledgeable or curious about the status of a Chicana in her own country. I can say with certainty, living as I do in a country where brown people are becoming more feared every day, that I have experienced more hostility toward Chicanas/os in a single day in the United States than I did in a year in Mexico.

During that time in Mexico, I was fortunate to meet, through a friend in Santa Cruz, a community of women professionals, activists, and artists. Through these women, I learned about the feminist movements in Mexico and was able to explore with them their perceptions of Chicano culture and Chicana culture, specifically.[5] Many of these women were familiar with Chicana literature through the works of Gloria Anzaldúa, Cherríe Moraga, Sandra Cisneros, Ana Castillo, and others. Some of these women had participated in *focos* (workshops) with Chicana writers and felt a bond with this marginalized group; this made my entrance into their community very welcoming.

I was fortunate to have the support of Dr. Eugenia Gaona, a Mexican scholar of Chicano literature. I was able to take an independent study with her and read the works of Rolando Hinojosa. It was wonderful to have her support and guidance in the early stages of my graduate career. In Mexico, I was continuing to trace the wonderful fluidity of Chicana/o authors in the United States who wrote about their experiences of being "ni de aquí, ni de allá," the in-between space of their existence. The literature traveled to Mexico and was examined by a Mexican scholar, then it was studied in Mexico by a Chicana who carried it back to a U.S. audience, and the bridge was extended. This transnational intellectual circulation of Chicana/o literature and criticism refutes the marginalization of these works in the academy today.

A new dimension to the transnationalism of Chicano literature was revealed unexpectedly when I received a Fulbright Fellowship the year before I earned tenure. As a senior Fulbright lecturer in American literature and cultures at the University of Málaga in southern Spain, I taught two courses: "North American Theater," and "U.S. Minority Literature." Being in a department of American literature scholars and feminist women in Spain was a very different experience from being in a predominantly male and social science–oriented home department in the United States. We experienced constant intellectual stimulation related to our shared training and work in American literatures. This created a political solidarity related to our work as feminists.

I had the opportunity to teach Chicano literature in both of my courses. Students welcomed this work as well as the accompanying critique of Spanish imperialism. Teaching mostly Spanish students, but also students from Scotland and England, affirmed for me the relevance of my project outside of the United States. I was contributing to the discourse of Transamerica in European studies. There is and has been a great interest in Chicano studies in Europe in general. Spain, in particular, has a community of scholars active in scholarship on Chicano literature and many students studying in the field.

Beyond the experience with students, and the smaller community of the university, there is a Chicano literature conference held biennially in Spain, which speaks again to the transnational nature of Chicano studies. While I was living and teaching in Málaga in 2004, I participated in the biennial Chicano Literature Conference held in Seville.

My two experiences living abroad—once as a student, once as a professor/scholar—have informed my thinking in ways that I know I have yet to discover. Most important have been the relationships that I developed. Some of the personal bonds that were created will last my entire life. My overall sense while in both Mexico and Spain was one of belonging.

My physical features allowed me to walk in both places unnoticed many times, even to appear as a local. This caused me to interrogate my own sense of boundaries, borders, history. Through all of this, my teaching improved and my scholarship was informed in new and exciting ways. I had to be especially careful about explaining history and terms for Spanish students, who did not have prior knowledge of the historical and cultural contexts explored in the literature they were reading. This gave me a new awareness of my students back at California State University, Long Beach, and the historical and cultural contexts that I sometimes took for granted but that they often lacked.

The experience of the Chicana has always been transnational. She has lived within and among many borders: geopolitical, spiritual, racial, ethnic, and sexual. In Mexico, my Lebanese friends from Juchitán, Oaxaca, understood Chicano identity through their own immigrant experience. In southern Spain, the experience of ethnic minorities became a point of departure for discussions about Chicano experiences.

It is because I entered this profession that I have been able to make the opportunities to research and teach abroad. I learned a great deal about myself through the experience of living abroad, and the places I lived—Mexico and Spain—connected me on a personal level to my experience. As a scholar, I was able to develop key *intercambios*. My personal and professional networks expanded. As an insider/outsider, I lived in that in-between space, the ambiguous space that Gloria Anzaldúa says gives us strength. As a traveler, my survival was dependent on my ability to straddle the borders I encountered daily. I called on Esperanza, La Llorona, the washerwoman, and La Salvaja to teach me to navigate and to be aware of the dangers in multiple spheres.[6]

These figures and what they symbolize inspire me daily to resist the oppression that I encounter in my profession. My aim has been to add to the cycle of learning by embracing the modes of resistance that Chicanas and Mexicanas practice while we live as teachers, scholars, and envoys. The transnational stories explored in these pages have both intellectual value and function as a form of productive practice, politics, and community.

# NOTES

1. When I was a student at UCSB in the mid-1980s, the Chicana/o Studies Department was a mid-size department and offered only a bachelor's degree. In 2005, it established a PhD program and accepted its first students in fall. Chicano and Latino studies departments nationwide are scarce. That the first PhD program in the discipline has only recently been established is disheartening, given the most recent census count of thirty million Hispanics in the United States.

CHAPTER ONE

1. See the epigraph in López-González, Malagamba, and Urrutia, eds., *Mujer y literatura mexicana y chicana:* "Con el deseo de unir los lazos entre las mujeres chicanas y mexicanas" [With the hope of binding the ties between Chicanas and Mexicanas] (7). Translations of this text in the chapter are by Cristina de la Torre.

2. I am making a distinction between the terms "Mexicana" and "Chicana." However, these acts of homogenization are being done for two very different reasons. For the U.S. government, merging the two terms is much like its imposition of the descriptor "Hispanic," a device used in census taking to erase or homogenize the many different groups in this country from Latin America. Yet, for the groups themselves the connection of the two terms, separated only by a

slash, is a statement pointing to political and cultural solidarity that attempts to unite them in order to bring a closer understanding of both worlds; it is not a form of governmental erasure. Also, it is only Chicanas who would make this gesture of joining the two terms, since a Chicana always has the Mexicana in her; the same is not true for the Mexicana.

3. See Anderson, *Imagined Communities*.

4. See Rebolledo and Rivero, eds., *Infinite Divisions*.

5. Ramon Saldívar explains in his introduction: "This narrative strategy for demystifying the relations between minority cultures and the dominant culture is the process I term 'the dialectics of difference' of Chicano literature. In the course of my discussion, I will show how the dialectical form of narratives by Chicano men and women is an authentic way of grappling with a reality that seems always to transcend representation, a reality into which the subject of the narrative's action seeks to enter, all the while learning the lesson of its own ideological closure, and of history's resistance to the symbolic structures in which subjectivity itself is formed." See *Chicano Narrative*, 5.

6. See Constantino, "Resistant Creativity"; Winkler, "Selected Mexicana and Chicana Fiction."

7. What I am calling comparative American studies refers to the United States and Latin America. I realize, however, that, although I am trying to be as inclusive as I can in my discussion, Canada is not examined in this work. Further comparative American studies need to include Canadian literature as well. There is a growing Salvadoran community in Canada, and the literature could be relevant to this study in looking at Latina writing across the hemisphere.

8. For a discussion of Latin American feminisms by Latin American feminists, see Saporta-Sternbach et al., "Feminisms in Latin America."

9. Studies by Anglo women like Castillo give an interesting viewpoint of Chicana, Latina, and Latin American feminist discourse that offers a very different representation of these feminisms from the analysis by those groups themselves.

10. This is Gustavo Pérez Firmat's term to refer to inter-American comparative studies.

11. Norma Alarcón gives a critique of the relationship between Chicana and Mexicana cultural production in "Cognitive Desires."

12. This parallels thematic developments in African American women's literature.

13. For an examination of feminist theory and the contributions of women of color, see hooks, *Talking Back: Thinking Feminist, Thinking Black*. Also see D. Castillo, *Talking Back: Toward a Latin American Feminist Literary Criticism*. I use the phrase "talking back" similarly to refer to Mexicanas and Chicanas talking back from the margins to the dominant patriarchal systems in their respective countries.

14. See Castellanos, *Mujer que sabe latín*, 7–21. Castellanos suggests that one is not born a Mexicana. I suggest that neither is one born a Chicana. Both are self-identified descriptors which assume a certain political ideology. See Alarcón, "Chicana Feminism."

15. As Deena González suggests, La Malinche can be viewed as the forerunner of Mexican women's liberation struggles. See "Encountering Columbus."

16. Also see Hidalgo, *Movimiento femenino en México*; Tuñes, *Mujeres en México*; Pérez, "Yucatecan Feminist Congress, 1917–18."

17. In 1848, with the annexation of nearly half of Mexico to the United States, Mexican-born citizens became U.S. citizens. See Del Castillo, *Between Borders*.

18. Again, here I refer mostly to historical studies. The bibliography of Chicana studies is extensive and continues to grow rapidly.

19. I will refer to the figure of La Malinche, the symbol, and to Malintzin, the actual historical figure, depending on the context of my discussion. Her Nahuatl birth name is Malintzin; in other contexts she is referred to as Malinal or Doña Marina, her Christian name.

20. See Anzaldúa, *Borderlands/La Frontera*. Here, Anzaldúa gives her interpretation of La Malinche when she writes, "Not me sold out my people, but they me," (22, 23) and she reads La Malinche as the woman who, to survive, acted as the interpreter for Hernán Cortés.

21. See Alcalá, "From Chingada to Chingona." In this essay, Alcalá offers an excellent critique of the historical La Malinche and her forgotten daughter, María Jaramillo. This reinsertion of Malinche's daughter, Alcalá argues, disrupts the "Mexicano/Chicano myth of mestizaje" (33).

22. Although the Llorona legend is more prevalent than La Malinche in popular culture, La Llorona is more adaptable for a children's tale. There may be a subconscious understanding of the figure of La Malinche in the tales of La Llorona. As adults, and especially during the Chicano Movement of the 1960s, "*malinchista*" became the name for a woman who was viewed as a traitor to the cause if she dared not submit to the sexism of the movement.

23. Translation by Alicia Jimenez.

24. See Saldívar-Hull, "Feminism on the Border."

25. One fifth of Chicana and Mexicana households always have been headed by women. See D. González, "The Widowed Women of Santa Fe."

26. See D. González, "Malinche as Lesbian."

## CHAPTER TWO

1. I do not want to suggest here that there ever was one model of family. The work of Chicana historians Emma Pérez, Antonia Castañeda, Irene Ledesma, and Deena González demonstrates that one fifth of households have always been headed by women. Chicanas are presenting this historical reality in their literature. See D. González, "The Widowed Women of Santa Fe."

2. Again, the same can be said of many Mexicana writers. Mexicana Elena Poniatowska believes the Chicana to be much more liberated in her thinking and therefore in the literary themes she addresses. For instance, she says that Chicanas have written much more on the subject of lesbian sexuality than have Mexicanas. In Mexico, a fear of ostracism for speaking out on lesbian issues, even the fear of imprisonment, is pervasive. See Poniatowska, "Puentes de ida y vuelta."

3. For further discussions of third world feminism, see Sandoval, "U.S. Third World Feminism." Since Sandoval's essay was published, there has been a shift from using the term "third world feminism." The methods that she outlines remain relevant even with the new terminology, however.

4. For other references to bridge feminism, see Anzaldúa and Keating, *This Bridge We Call Home.*

5. See Said, "Traveling Theory."

6. For other readings of Sandra Cisneros's *The House on Mango Street,* see Olivares, "Sandra Cisneros' *The House on Mango Street*"; Rosaldo, *Culture and Truth,* 160–170; idem, "Fables of the Fallen Guy"; R. Saldívar, *Chicano Narrative,* 171–199; Saldívar-Hull, "Mujeres en Lucha/Mujeres de Fuerza."

7. For the risks and attendant ramifications of telling secrets, see D. González, "Speaking Secrets."

8. This is a reference to Virginia Woolf's *A Room of One's Own.* Woolf, a middle-class Englishwoman, was able to imagine having her own personal space to create fiction. Esperanza, while living in

a home where the bathroom is shared by many families, is still able to dream of a house of her own—her own personal space in which to write and, more important, in which to live without a patriarchal presence.

9. The Virgin of Guadalupe is one symbol of the generational suffering that the protagonist Esperanza refers to. While many Chicana scholars have described the Virgin as a model of suffering, sacrifice, and servility, others have considered her a liberating figure and a symbol of resistance. See Rodríguez, *Our Lady of Guadalupe*.

10. The mango can also be understood here as a symbol of a budding sexuality. Esperanza feminizes Mango Street. Also, in Asian Indian cultures, the mango is a sign of fertility and good fortune.

11. For another discussion of "Beautiful and Cruel," see McCracken, "Sandra Cisneros' *The House on Mango Street*."

12. See Pérez, "Sexuality and Discourse."

13. For Chicana revisions of La Llorona in fiction, see Gaspar de Alba, Herrera-Sobek, and Martínez, "Beggar on the Córdova Bridge"; G. Limón, *In Search of Bernabé*.

14. Here I am arguing against the masculinist readings of La Llorona and the significance of water imagery in the traditional versions of this cultural symbol.

15. Franco primarily discusses popular narrative in this essay, yet she states that "many other sub-genres of narrative for women, many of which—the *libro semanal,* the television soap opera, and type of photo novel known as *novelas rojas*—can no longer be classified as romance. Indeed, because they present such a violent contrast to romance"; see *Plotting Women,* 124. Cisneros's narrative presents this contrast as Cleófilas chooses in the end to escape her oppressors, both her husband and the United States, by crossing the border.

16. El Grito de Dolores originated during the Mexican war of Independence from Spain. A revolutionary priest from the state of Guanajuato, Miguel Hidalgo, "pealed the bells of the church of Dolores to summon the Indians to fight for their freedom"; see Galeano, "A Flood of Tears and Blood," 9. El Grito de Dolores is reenacted every year on the sixteenth of September to commemorate Mexico's independence.

17. A lesbian critique would present Felice as an object of desire for Cleófilas and would see Felice as a seductress. Felice becomes Cleófilas's Prince Charming as she rescues her from a terrible fate. Cleófilas is fascinated by Felice, as she is fascinated by La Llorona.

La Gritona (Felice) becomes not only Cleófilas's opportunity to cross the geographical border between the United States and Mexico, but also her opportunity for a sexual border crossing if we read Felice as a lesbian. For one lesbian rereading of the Llorona legend, see Palacios, "La Llorona Loca." In Palacios' comical story, La Llorona, The Crazy Crier, kills her female lover, La Stranger, in a fit of jealousy and can be heard crying every night for La Stranger.

18. For another reading of "Woman Hollering Creek," see D. González, "Sandra Cisneros' *Woman Hollering Creek*."

19. A *coyote* is a person who assists someone without documentation to cross the border. Very often, *coyotes* will take advantage of their "client" financially, psychologically, and physically. Women are sometimes raped, and, because of their circumstances, they have no recourse. Felice is a compassionate *coyote* and aids Cleófilas in her liberation rather than abusing her.

20. Since the 1970s, Chicana visual artists have been involved in the process of reimagining Mexican female cultural archetypes. Some of those images include Ester Hernández's "La Virgen de Guadalupe defendiendo los derechos de los Chicanos," which depicts a Chicana as a martial artist. Yolanda López has produced a trilogy of revisions of La Virgen de Guadalupe. López paints herself as marathon runner, her mother as a garment worker, and her grandmother as sitting up resting. There are many artists who have reworked these archetypes in order to give themselves and other Chicanas something tangible to relate to, ordinary women with extraordinary stories. The most recent images by a Chicana artist are the "Lupe and Sirena" series produced by Alma López in which she honors La Virgen de Guadalupe by transforming her into a sensual woman, realistic and meaningful to the artist.

## CHAPTER THREE

1. The 1980s falls between what are referred to as the "boom" and the "postboom" phases in Mexican literature.

2. Aware of the biases that exist, I was surprised to find a course in Mexico in which I first had the opportunity to read two of the authors whom I discuss in this chapter. The course was titled "Literatura Femenina," and the texts included works by Mexican authors Rosario Castellanos, Elena Garro, Inés Arredondo, Josefina Vicéns, Silvia Molina, Rosa María Roffiel, Carmen Boullosa, and Laura Esquivel. The enrollment was small compared with that of other, more

mainstream, courses and half of the students were from California. The instructor did not consider herself a feminist, but her pedagogy and methodology were feminist-centered. The course was unique in that it was one of the few, if not the only, class that dealt exclusively with contemporary women's literature. A graduate course focused on the work of Sor Juana Inés de la Cruz.

My experience in a theory course was very different. I recall the professor taunting me in class for the focus of my class project, women's literature. While many students and faculty welcomed my interest in and attention to Mexicana writing, and the larger project of comparing Chicana and Mexicana writing, there were always those who believed that I really ought to have been examining the more "serious and important authors," that is, the canon of male authors.

3. See Walker, *In Search of Our Mothers' Gardens*.

4. For examples, see *Teatro herético* (1987), a compilation of three parodies in play format—*Aura y las once mil vírgenes, Cocinar hombres*, and *Propusieron a María*—also, *Ingobernable*.

5. For a discussion of portrayals of "bad women" in Chicana literature, see Rebolledo, *Women Singing in the Snow*, 183–206.

6. See Cisneros, *My Wicked, Wicked Ways*.

7. Carmen Boullosa is a recipient of the Premio Xavier Villaurrutia (1989), one of Mexico's most prestigious literary awards, for her novel *Antes*, her poetry collection *La Salvaja*, and her essays *Papeles irresponsables*.

8. Boullosa's novels have piqued the interest of critics more than her early short fiction, theater, and poetry. *Leaving Tabasco* (2001), *They're Cows, We're Pigs* (1997), and *Cleopatra Dismounts* (2003) have all been translated and published in the United States.

9. Translations of Boullosa's works in this chapter by Cristina de la Torre.

10. *Loose Woman* and *My Wicked, Wicked Ways* present women who constantly challenge the boundaries of womanhood.

11. For a critique of *Mother, May I?*, see Passman, "Demeter, Kore and the Birth of the Self." Also see M. Sánchez, *Contemporary Chicana Poetry*, 24–84.

12. For another analysis of *Mejor desaparece*, see García-Serrano, "Sí, mejor desaparece de Carmen Boullosa." Also see Monzón, "Algunos aspectos de la metaficción en *Mejor desaparece*." For criticism of other Boullosa works, see Droescher and Rincón, *Acercamientos a Carmen Boullosa*.

13. See the following critical articles on the novel and film: Glenn,

"Postmodern Parody and Culinary Narrative Art in Laura Esquivel's *Como agua para chocolate*"; B. González, "Para comerte mejor"; Kraniauskas, review of *Como agua para chocolate*; Lawless, "Experimental Cooking in *Como agua para chocolate*"; Lillo, "El reciclaje del melodrama y sus repercusiones en la estratificación de la cultura"; Marquet, "¿Como escribir un best-seller?; Oropesa, "*Como agua para chocolate* de Laura Esquivel"; Schmidt, "La risa"; Segovia, "Only Cauldrons Know the Secrets of Their Soups."

14. Unless otherwise noted, this text refers to the English edition of the novel, translated by Carol Christenson and Thomas Christenson.

15. See Zeff, "'What Doesn't Kill You, Makes You Fat.'"

16. Kickapoo is part of the Algonquian family of languages, spoken in Kansas, Oklahoma, and northern Mexico. The Kickapoo people originated in the Michigan-Illinois homeland but resisted European colonization. Many migrated southward to Texas and Mexico, the border between which is where Dr. John Brown resides in the novel. Kickapoo culture and language are most traditional in Mexico. Dr. Brown adopts his Kickapoo grandmother's traditional healing methods and combines them with his training in western medicine.

17. See Alcoff, "Cultural Feminism Versus Post-Structuralism." Alcoff addresses some differences in liberal feminism and cultural feminism when stating: "After a decade of liberal feminists advising us to wear business suits and enter the male world, it is a helpful corrective to have cultural feminists argue instead that women's world is full of superior virtues and values, to be credited and learned from rather than despised" (414).

CHAPTER FOUR

An earlier version of chapter 4 appears as "Forming Feminist Coalitions: The Internationalist Agenda of Helena María Viramontes," *Chicana Literary and Artistic Expressions,* Maria Herrera-Sobek, ed. © 2000, pp. 77–91. Reprinted with the permission of the Center for Chicano Studies Publication Series, UCSB.

1. Introduction from Mohanty, Russo, and Torres, eds., *Third World Women,* 7.

2. For an articulation of the analytical categories for "making theory," see Anzaldúa, ed., *Making Face, Making Soul.*

3. The proposition passed with 58.8 percent of the vote. The fed-

eral courts overturned it because it exceeded the state's authority in a federal realm—immigration.

4. Many of her characters are talking back to the dominant white colonialist culture. Her Chicana characters are also responding to their own Chicano culture.

5. The role of scribe is one which many Chicanas have adopted, not only as adults but as children as well. See Moraga, *Loving in the War Years*; Cervantes, *Emplumada*.

6. Viramontes, *The Moths and Other Stories*. Page references are to this edition.

7. One avenue for Chicanas and other women of color to publish their work is edited anthologies, which create a coalition across cultural and ethnic identities. There are also journals which specialize in Chicana/o issues and women's issues.

8. Debra Castillo would argue against this interpretation. In her reading of this short story, she presumes the national identity of the characters, which I believe limits the reading of this story as a narrative of the Americas. See *Talking Back*, 71–95.

9. See G. Limón, *In Search of Bernabé*. Limón's novel is another example of La Llorona traveling throughout America in search of her child. The protagonist travels between Los Angeles and El Salvador to look for her son, who went missing during the war in El Salvador.

10. This is a reference to Woolf, *A Room of One's Own*. The title of this book written by a wealthy British woman represents the basic necessities that Viramontes's characters desire. They would be happy just not sharing a toilet with several other families; the luxury of having a room of one's own room is unthinkable.

11. I refer here to the traditional U.S. ideals of honesty that have always been in contradiction to the government's actions, for example, the breaking of the treaties with the Native Americans. See Churchill, *Struggle for the Land*.

12. See L. Chávez, *Shadowed Lives*.

13. See Tula, *Hear My Testimony*.

14. See Ruiz, "'And Miles to Go . . .'" Also see Martínez and McCaughan, "Chicanas and Mexicanas within a Transnational Working Class."

15. This has created an increase in anti-immigrant sentiment. As a result, a significant immigrant-rights movement has developed in major cities across the United States.

1. See Paulo Freire, Myra Bergman Ramon, (translator) Donaldo Macedo. New York: Continuum. 2000.

2. Marisol Moreno's forthcoming doctoral thesis, "Of the Community, For the Community: The Chicana and Chicano Movement in Southern California's Public Higher Education, 1967–1973" is adding to these feminist critiques of Chicano nationalism.

3. In *Feminist Theory from Margin to Center,* bell hooks calls for bringing men into the struggle for women's liberation. This is a common thread among many feminists of color. The women and men in the ongoing ethnicity-based political movements must recognize this call as a key component in their efforts.

4. See Anzaldúa, *Borderlands/La Frontera,* 19–20.

5. Such encounters are not always positive. For other attempts at community building between Mexicanas and Chicanas, see M. Chávez, "Pilgrimage to the Motherland: California Chicanas and International Women's Year, Mexico City, 1975," in Vicki Ruiz and John Chavez, eds., *Memories and Migrations: Mapping Boricua/ Chicana Histories.*

6. These are all literary characters which are discussed in Chapters 2, 3, and 4. All of these figures live in a state of constant resistance as a means of survival.

# BIBLIOGRAPHY

Alarcón, Norma. "Chicana Feminism: In the Tracks of the 'Native Woman.'" *Cultural Studies* 4, no. 3 (1990): 248–256.

———. "Chicana's Feminist Literature: A Revision through Malintzin/or Malintzin: Putting Flesh Back on the Object." In *This Bridge Called My Back: Writings by Radical Women of Color*, ed. Cherríe Moraga and Gloria Anzaldúa, 182–190. Watertown, Mass.: Persephone Press, 1981.

———. "Cognitive Desires: An Allegory of/for Chicana Critics." In *Chicana (W)rites: On Word and Film*, ed. María Herrera-Sobek and Helena María Viramontes, 185–200. Berkeley, Calif.: Third Woman Press, 1995.

———. "Making Familia from Scratch: Split Subjectivities in the Work of Helena María Viramontes and Cherríe Moraga." *The Americas Review* 15 (Fall–Winter 1987): 147–159.

———. "The Theoretical Subject(s) in *This Bridge Called My Back* and Anglo-American Feminism." *Criticism in the Borderlands: Studies in Chicano Literature*, ed. José Saldívar and Héctor Calderón, 28–39. Durham, N.C.: Duke University Press, 1991.

———. "Traddutora, Traditora: A Paradigmatic Figure of Chicana Feminism." *Cultural Critique* (Fall 1989): 57–87.

———. "What Kind of Lover Have You Made Me Mother?: Towards a Theory of Chicana's Feminism and Cultural Identity Through Poetry." In *Women of Color: Perspectives on Feminism and Identity*, ed. Audrey T. McCluskey. Women's Studies Program Occasional Papers Series 1, no. 1. Bloomington: Indiana University, 1985.

Alarcón, Norma, Ana Castillo, and Cherríe Moraga, eds. *Third Woman: The Sexuality of Latinas*. Berkeley, Calif.: Third Woman Press, 1989.

Alcalá, Rita Cano. "From Chingada to Chingona: La Malinche

Redefined or, a Long Line of Hermanas." *Aztlán* 26, no. 2 (Fall 2001): 33–61.

Alcoff, Linda "Cultural Feminism Versus Post-Structuralism: The Identity Crisis in Feminist Theory." *Signs: Journal of Women in Culture and Society* 13, no. 3 (1988): 405–436.

Anaya, Rudolfo. *Bless Me, Última.* Berkeley: Tonatiuh–Quinto Sol International, 1972.

Anderson, Benedict. *Imagined Communities: Reflections on the Origin and Spread of Nationalism.* New York: Verso, 1991.

Anzaldúa, Gloria. *Borderlands/La Frontera.* San Francisco: Spinsters/Aunt Lute, 1987.

———, ed. *Making Face, Making Soul=Haciendo Caras: Creative and Critical Perspectives by Women of Color.* San Francisco: Aunt Lute Foundation Books, 1990.

Anzaldúa, Gloria, and Analouise Keating, eds. *This Bridge We Call Home: Radical Visions for Transformation.* New York: Routledge, 2004.

Anzaldúa, Gloria, and Cherríe Moraga, eds. *This Bridge Called My Back: Writings by Radical Women of Color.* Watertown, Mass.: Persephone Press, 1981; 2nd ed. New York: Kitchen Table Press, 1983.

Bartlett, Catherine Vallejos. "Breaking Taboos: Positive and Negative Sexuality in Chicana Literature." MA thesis, University of New Mexico, 1986.

Boullosa, Carmen. *Antes.* Mexico City: Vuelta, 1989.

———. *Cleopatra Dismounts.* Trans. Geoff Hargreaves. New York: Grove Press, 2002.

———. *Leaving Tabasco.* Trans. Geoff Hargreaves. New York: Grove Press, 2002.

———. *Mejor desaparece.* Mexico City: Oceano, 1987.

———. *La salvaja.* Mexico City: Fondo de Cultura Económica, 1989.

———. *Son vacas, somos puercos: Filibusteros del Mar Caribe.* Mexico City: Ediciones Era, 1991.

———. *They're Cows, We're Pigs.* Trans. Leland H. Chambers. New York: Grove Press, 2001.

Broyles-González, Yolanda. *El Teatro Campesino: Theater in the Chicano Movement.* Austin: University of Texas Press, 1994.

Calderón, Héctor. "At the Crossroads of History, on the Borders of Change: Chicano Literary Studies Past, Present, and Future." In *Left Politics and the Literary Profession,* ed. Lennard J. Davis and M. Bella Mirabella, 211–235. New York: Columbia University Press, 1990.

Candelaria, Cordelia. "La Malinche, Feminist Prototype." *Frontiers* 5, no. 2 (1980): 1–6.

Castañeda, Antonia I. "Engendering the History of Alta California, 1769–1848: Gender, Sexuality, and the Family." In Contested Eden: California Before the Gold Rush, ed. Ramon Gutierrez and Richard J. Orsi, 230–259. Berkeley: University of California Press, 1998.

———. "Women of Color and the Rewriting of Western History: The Discourse, Politics, and Decolonization of History." Special issue: *Pacific Historical Review* 61, no. 4 (1992).

Castellanos, Rosario. *Álbum de familia.* 2nd ed. Mexico City: J. Mortiz, 1975.

———. *El eterno femenino: Farsa.* Mexico City: Fondo de Cultura Económica, 1975.

———. *Mujer que sabe latín.* Mexico City: Fondo de Cultura Económica, 1984.

Castillo, Ana. *Massacre of the Dreamers.* Albuquerque: University of New Mexico Press, 1994.

———. *The Mixquiahuala Letters.* Binghamton, N.Y.: Bilingual Press/Editorial Bilingüe, 1986.

Castillo, Debra. *Talking Back: Toward a Latin American Feminist Literary Criticism.* Ithaca, N.Y.: Cornell University Press, 1992.

Castillo-Speed, Lillian. *Latina: Women's Voices from the Borderlands.* New York: Simon & Schuster, 1995.

Cervantes, Lorna Dee. *Emplumada.* Pittsburgh: University of Pittsburgh Press, 1981.

Chabram, Angie. "Chicano Critical Discourse: An Emerging Cultural Practice." *Aztlán* 18, no. 2 (Fall 1987): 45–90.

———. "'I Throw Punches for My Race, but I Don't Want to Be a Man': Writing Us—Chica-nos (Girl, Us)/Chicanas—Into the Movement Script." In *Cultural Studies*, ed. Lawrence Grossberg, Cary Nelson, and Paula Treichler, 81–95. New York: Routledge, 1992.

Chabram, Angie, and Rosalinda Fregoso, eds. "Chicana/o Cultural Representations: Reframing Critical Discourses." Special issue: *Cultural Studies* 4, no. 3 (1990).

Chávez, Denise. *Face of an Angel.* New York: Farrar, Straus & Giroux, 1994.

Chávez, Leo. *Shadowed Lives: Undocumented Immigrants in American Society.* New York: Harcourt Brace, 1992.

Chávez, Maricela R. "Pilgrimage to the Motherland: California Chacanas and International Women's Year, Mexico City, 1975." In *Memories and Migrations: Mapping Boricua/Chicana Histories,* eds. Vicki Ruiz and John Chávez. Champaign: University of Illinois Press, 2008.

Chevigny, Bell, and Gari Laguardia, eds. *Reinventing the Americas: Comparative Studies of Literature of the United States and Spanish America.* New York: Cambridge University Press, 1986.

Christian, Barbara. *Black Feminist Criticism: Perspectives on Black Women Writers.* New York: Pergamon Press, 1985.

Churchill, Ward. *Struggle for the Land: Indigenous Resistance to Genocide, Ecocide and Expropriation in Contemporary North America.* Monroe, Maine: Common Courage Press, 1993.

Cisneros, Sandra. *The House on Mango Street.* Houston, Tex.: Arte Público Press, 1984; 2nd rev. ed. New York: Random House, 1988.

———. *Loose Woman.* New York: Knopf, 1994.

———. *My Wicked, Wicked Ways.* Berkeley: Third Woman Press, 1987; New York: Turtle Bay, 1992.

———. *Woman Hollering Creek and Other Stories.* New York: Random House, 1990.

Constantino, Roselyn. "Resistant Creativity: Interpretative Strategies and Gender Representation in Contemporary Women's Writing in Mexico." PhD diss., Arizona State University, 1992.

Córdova, Teresa. "Roots & Resistance: The Emergent Writings of Twenty Years of Chicana Feminist Struggle." In *Handbook of Hispanic Cultures in the United States: Sociology,* ed. Félix Padilla, 175–202. Houston, Tex.: Arte Público Press, 1994.

Córdova, Teresa, Norma Cantú, Gilberto Cárdenas, Juan García, and Christine M. Sierra, eds. *Chicana Voices: Intersections of Class, Race and Gender.* Austin, Tex.: Center for Mexican American Studies, 1986.

Cotera, Martha P. *The Chicana Feminist.* Austin, Tex.: Information Systems Development, 1977.

———. *Diosa y Hembra: The History and Heritage of Chicanas in the U.S.* Austin, Tex.: Information Systems Development, 1976.

Cypess, Sandra. *La Malinche in Mexican Literature: From History to Myth.* Austin: University of Texas Press, 1991.

de la Torre, Alela, and Beatriz M. Pesquera, eds. *Building with Our*

*Hands: Directions in Chicana Studies*. Berkeley & Los Angeles: University of California Press, 1993.

de Lauretis, Teresa, ed. *Feminist Studies, Critical Studies*. Bloomington: Indiana University Press, 1986.

Del Castillo, Adelaida R., ed. *Between Borders: Essays on Mexicana/ Chicana History*. Encino, Calif.: Floricanto Press, 1990.

Droescher, Barbara, and Carlos Rincón. *Acercamientos a Carmen Boullosa*. Berlin: Edition Arena, 1999.

Eger, Ernestina N. *A Bibliography of Criticism of Contemporary Chicano Literature*. Chicano Studies Library Publications Series, no. 5. Berkeley: University of California Chicano Studies Library Publications, 1982.

Esquivel, Laura. *Como agua para chocolate: Novela de entregas mensuales con recetas, amores y remedios caseros*. México D. F.: Editorial Planeta Mexicana, 1989.

———. *Like Water for Chocolate: A Novel in Monthly Installments, with Recipes, Romances, and Home Remedies*. Trans. Carol Christensen and Thomas Christensen. New York: Doubleday, 1992.

Eysturoy, Annie Olivia. "Narratives of Self: The Chicana Bildungsroman/Kunstlerroman." PhD diss., University of New Mexico, 1994.

Fisher, Dexter, ed. *The Third Woman: Minority Women Writers of The United States*. Boston: Houghton Mifflin, 1980.

Foppa, Adelaida. "Feminismo y liberación." In *Imagen y realidad de la mujer*, ed. Elena Urrutia, 80–101. Mexico City: SepSetentas, 1975.

Franco, Jean. *Plotting Women: Gender and Representation in Mexico*. New York: Columbia University Press, 1989.

Friere, Paolo. *Pedagogy of the Oppressed*. Trans. Myra Bergman Ramon. New York: Continuum Publishing Company, 1989.

Friedman, Thomas. *The Lexus and the Olive Tree*. New York: Farrar, Straus & Giroux, 1999.

Galarza, Ernesto. *Barrio Boy: The Story of a Boy's Acculturation*. Notre Dame, Ind.: Notre Dame University Press, 1980.

Galeano, Eduardo. "A Flood of Tears and Blood: And Yet the Pope Said Indians Had Souls." In *Eating Fire, Tasting Blood: An Anthology of the American Indian Holocaust*. Ed. Marijo Moore. New York: Thunder's Mountain Press, 2006. 1–15.

García, Alma. "The Development of Chicana Feminist Discourse, 1970–1980." *Gender and Society* 3, no. 2 (1989): 217–238.

García-Serrano, María Victoria. "Sí, mejor desaparece de Carmen Boullosa: ¿Una versión de la loca criolla en el ático?" *Texto Crítico* 5, no. 10 (Jan.–June 2002): 145–157.

Garfield, Evelyn Picon. *Women's Voices from Latin America: Interviews With Six Contemporary Authors.* Detroit, Mich.: Wayne State University Press, 1985.

Garro, Elena. *Los recuerdos del porvenir.* 1st ed. Mexico City: J. Mortiz, 1987.

Gaspar de Alba, Alicia, María Herrera-Sobek, and Demetria Martínez. "Beggar on the Cordova Bridge." In *Three Times a Woman: Chicana Poetry,* ed. Alicia Gaspar de Alba, María Herrera-Sobek, and Demetria Martínez. Tempe, Ariz.: Bilingual Press, 1989.

——. *The Mystery of Survival.* Tempe, Ariz.: Bilingual Press, 1993.

Gibbons, Reginald, ed. "New Writing from Mexico." Special issue: *Triquarterly* (Fall 1992).

Giménez Caballero, Ernesto. *Las mujeres de América.* Madrid: Editora Nacional, 1971.

Glenn, Cathleen M. "Postmodern Parody and Culinary Narrative Art in Laura Esquivel's *Como agua para chocolate.*" *Chasqui: Revista de Literatura Latinoamericana* 23, no. 2 (1994): 39–47.

Gómez, Alma, Cherríe Moraga, and Mariana Romo-Carmona, eds. *Cuentos: Stories by Latinas.* New York: Kitchen Table, Women of Color Press, 1983.

González, Beatriz. "Para comerte mejor: Cultura calibanesca y formas literarias alternativas." *Nuevo Texto Crítico* 5, no. 9–10 (1992): 201–215.

González, Deena. "Encountering Columbus." In *Chicano Studies: Critical Connection between Research and Community,* ed. Teresa Córdova. National Association of Chicano Studies, 1992.

——. "Malinche as Lesbian: A Reconfiguration of 500 Years of Resistance." Special issue: *California Sociologist* 14, nos. 1–2 (1991).

——. "Sandra Cisneros' *Woman Hollering Creek.*" Pomona College, Claremont, Calif., 1994.

——. "Speaking Secrets: Living Chicana Theory." In *Living Chicana Theory,* ed. Carla Trujillo, 46–77. Berkeley, Calif.: Third Woman Press, 1998.

——. "The Widowed Women of Santa Fe: Assessments on the Lives of an Unmarried Population, 1850–1880." In *Unequal Sisters,* ed. Ellen DuBois and Vicki Ruiz, 65–90. New York: Routledge, 1990.

González, Rodolpho. *Yo soy Joaquín: An Epic Poem.* New York: Bantam Books, 1972.

González-Berry, Erlinda, and Tey Diana Rebolledo. "Growing Up Chicano: Tomás Rivera and Sandra Cisneros." *International Studies in Honor of Tomás Rivera*, ed. Julián Olivares, 109–119. Houston: Arte Público Press, 1985.

Gutiérrez-Jones, Carl Scott. *Rethinking Borderlands: Between Chicano Culture and Legal Discourse.* Berkeley & Los Angeles: University of California Press, 1995.

Harlow, Barbara. *Resistance Literature.* New York: Methuen, 1987.

Harrington, Michael. *The Next America: The Decline and Rise of the United States.* New York: Holt, Rinehart & Winston, 1981.

———. *The Other America: Poverty in the United States.* New York: Macmillan, 1962.

Herrera-Sobek, María, ed. *Beyond Stereotypes: The Critical Analysis of Chicana Literature.* Binghamton, N.Y.: Bilingual Press, 1985.

———. *Reconstructing a Chicana/o Literary Heritage: Hispanic Colonial Literature of the Southwest.* Tucson: University of Arizona Press, 1993.

Herrera-Sobek, María, and Helena María Viramontes, eds. "Chicana Creativity and Criticism: Charting New Frontiers in American Literature." Special issue: *The Americas Review* 15 (1987): 3–4.

Hidalgo, Berta. *Movimiento femenino en México.* Mexico City: Editores Asociados Mexicanos, 1980.

hooks, bell. *Feminist Theory from Margin to Center.* Boston: South End Press, 1984.

———. *Talking Back: Thinking Feminist, Thinking Black.* Boston: South End Press, 1989.

Horno-Delgado, Asunción, Eliana Ortega, Nina M. Scott, and Nancy Saporta Sternbach, eds. *Breaking Boundaries: Latina Writing and Critical Readings.* Amherst: University of Massachusetts Press, 1989.

Hurtado, Aida. "Relating to Privilege: Seduction and Rejection in the Subordination of White Women and Women of Color." *Signs: Journal of Women in Culture and Society* 14, no. 4 (1989): 833–855.

Jayawardena, Kumari. *Feminism and Nationalism in the Third World.* London: Zed Books, 1986.

Jussawalla, Feroza. *Interviews with Writers of the Post-Colonial World*. Jackson: University Press of Mississippi, 1992.

King, Martin Luther, Jr. *A Testament of Hope: The Essential Writings of Martin Luther King Jr.*, ed. James Melvin Washington. San Francisco: Harper & Row, 1986.

Kraniauskas, John. Review of *Como agua para chocolate*, dir. Alfonso Arau. *Sight and Sound* 3, no. 10 (Oct. 1993): 42.

Küppers, Gaby, ed. *Compañeras: Voices from the Latin American Women's Movement*. London: Latin American Bureau, 1994.

LaDuke, Betty. *Compañeras: Women, Art, & Social Change in Latin America*. San Francisco: City Lights Books, 1985.

Lamas, Marta, et al., eds. "Amor y democracia." Special issue: *Debate Feminista* (March 1990).

Lawless, Cecilia. "Experimental Cooking in *Como agua para chocolate*." *Monographic Review* 8 (1992): 261–272.

Leal, Luis. "Literary Criticism and Minority Literatures: The Case of the Chicano Writer." *Confluencia: Revista Hispánica de Cultura y Literatura* 1, no. 2, (Spring 1986): 4–9.

Lillo, Gastón. "El reciclaje del melodrama y sus repercusiones en la estratificación de la cultura." *Archivos de la Filmoteca: Revista de Estudios Históricos sobre la Imagen* (1994): 65–73.

Limón, Graciela. *In Search of Bernabé*. Houston, Tex.: Arte Público Press, 1993.

Limón, José. "La Llorona, the Third Legend of Greater Mexico: Cultural Symbols, Women, and the Political Unconscious." *Renato Rosaldo Lecture Series Monograph* 2 (Spring 1986): 59–93.

Lomas, Clara. "Mexican Precursors of Chicana Feminist Writing." In *Multiple Literature of the United States: Critical Introductions and Classroom Resources*, ed. Cordelia Candelaria, 21–33. Boulder: University of Colorado, 1989.

López-González, Aralia, Amelia Malagamba, and Elena Urrutia, eds. *Mujer y literatura mexicana y chicana: Culturas en contacto*. 2 vols. Mexico City: Colegio de México, Programa Interdisciplinario de Estudios de la Mujer; Tijuana, B.C.: Colegio de la Frontera Norte, 1988, 1990.

Lorde, Audre. *Sister/Outsider*. New York: The Crossing Press, 1984.

Macías, Anna. *Against All Odds: The Feminist Movement in Mexico to 1940*. Westport, Conn.: Greenwood Press: 1982.

Manguel, Alberto, ed. *Other Fires: Short Fiction by Latin American Women*. New York: Clarkson N. Potter, 1986.

Marquet, Antonio. "¿Como escribir un best-seller? La receta de Laura Esquivel." *Plural: Revista Cultural de Excélsior* (1991): 58–67.

Martí, José. *The America of José Martí: Selected Writings*, trans. Juan de Onís. New York: Noonday Press, 1953.

———. *Inside the Monster: Writings on the United States and American Imperialism*, trans. Elinor Randall. New York: Monthly Review Press, 1975.

Martínez, Elizabeth, and Ed McCaughan. "Chicanas and Mexicanas within a Transnational Working Class." In *Between Borders: Essays on Mexicana/Chicana History*, 31–60. Encino, Calif.: Floricanto Press, 1990.

Mastretta, Ángeles. *Arráncame la vida*. Mexico City: Ediciones Oceano, 1986.

McCracken, Ellen. "Sandra Cisneros' *The House on Mango Street*: Community-oriented Introspection and the Demystification of Patriarchal Violence." In *Breaking Boundaries: Latina Writing and Critical Readings,* ed. Asunción Horno-Delgado et al., 62–71. Amherst: University of Massachusetts Press, 1989.

Meyer, Doris, and Margarite Fernández Olmos, eds. *Contemporary Women Authors of Latin America*. Brooklyn, N.Y.: Brooklyn College Press, 1981.

Miller, Beth. *Mujeres en la literatura*. Mexico City: Fleischer, 1978.

Mirandé, Alfredo, and Evangelina Enríquez. *La Chicana: The Mexican American Woman*. Chicago: University of Chicago Press, 1979.

Mohanty, Chandra Talpade, Ann Russo, and Lourdes Torres, eds. *Third World Women and the Politics of Feminism*. Bloomington: Indiana University Press, 1991.

Monzón, Lorena. "Algunos aspectos de la metaficción en *Mejor desaparece*." *Revista de Literatura Mexicana Contemporánea* 8, no. 15 (Jan.–Apr. 2002): 39–45

Mora, Magdelena and Adelaida Del Castillo, eds. *Mexican Women in the U.S.: Struggles Past and Present*. Los Angeles: Chicano Studies Research Center Publications. University of California, 1980.

Moraga, Cherríe. *Giving Up the Ghost*. Los Angeles: West End Press, 1986.

———. *Loving in the War Years*. Boston: South End Press, 1983.

Moreno, Marisol. "Of the Community, For the Community: The Chicana and Chicano Student Movement in Southern California's

Public Higher Education, 1967–1973." Diss. University of California, Santa Barbara. Forthcoming 2008.

Niranjana, Tejaswini. *Siting Translation: History, Post-Structuralism, and the Colonial Context.* Berkeley & Los Angeles: University of California Press, 1992.

Olivares, Julián. "Sandra Cisneros' *The House on Mango Street,* and the Poetics of Space." In *Chicana Creativity and Criticism: Charting New Frontiers in American Literature,* ed. María Herrera-Sobek and Helena María Viramontes, 160–170. Houston, Tex.: Arte Público Press, 1987.

Ordóñez, Elizabeth J. "Sexual Politics and the Theme of Sexuality in Chicana Poetry." In *Women in Hispanic Literature: Icons and Fallen Idols,* ed. Beth Miller, 316–319. Berkeley & Los Angeles: University of California Press, 1983.

Oropesa, Salvador A. "*Como agua para chocolate* de Laura Esquivel como lectura del manual de urbanidad y buenas costumbres de Manuel Antonio Carreno." *Monographic Review* 8 (1992): 252–260.

Palacios, Monica. "La Llorona Loca: The Other Side." In *Chicana Lesbians: The Girls Our Mothers Warned Us About,* ed. Carla Trujillo, 49–51. Berkeley, Calif.: Third Woman Press, 1991.

Parkinson Zamora, Lois. *Writing the Apocalypse: Historical Vision in Contemporary U.S. and Latin American Fiction.* Cambridge: Cambridge University Press, 1989.

Passman, Kristina. "Demeter, Kore and the Birth of the Self: The Quest for Identity in the Poetry of Alma Villanueva, Pat Mora, and Cherríe Moraga." *Monographic Review/Revista Monográfica* 6 (1990): 323–342.

Paz, Octavio, *The Labyrinth of Solitude: Life and Thought in Mexico.* New York: Grove Press, 1961.

Pérez, Emma. "Sexuality and Discourse: Notes from a Chicana Survivor." In *Chicana Lesbians: The Girls Our Mothers Warned Us About,* ed. Carla Trujillo, 159–184. Berkeley, Calif.: Third Woman Press, 1991.

———. "Yucatecan Feminist Congress, 1917–1918." PhD diss., University of California, Los Angeles, 1988.

Pérez Firmat, Gustavo, ed. *Do the Americas Have a Common Literature?* Durham, N.C.: Duke University Press, 1990.

Poniatowska, Elena. *Hasta no verte Jesús mío.* Mexico City: Lecturas Mexicanas, 1969.

——. "La literatura de las mujeres es parte de la literatura de los oprimidos." *Fem* 6, no. 21 (1982): 23–27.

——. "Mexicanas and Chicanas." *MELUS* 21, no. 3, Other Americas (Autumn 1996): 35–51.

——. "Puentes de ida y vuelta." *La Jornada* 5, no. 246 (1989): 2–5.

Quintana, Alvina E. *Home Girls: Chicana Literary Voices.* Philadelphia: Temple University Press, 1995.

Radway, Janice A. *Reading the Romance: Women, Patriarchy, and Popular Literature.* Chapel Hill: University of North Carolina Press, 1991.

Rebolledo, Tey Diana. "Abuelitas: Mythology and Integration in Chicana Literature." In *Woman of Her Word: Hispanic Women Write,* ed. Evangelina Vigil, 148–158. Houston, Tex.: Arte Público Press, 1983.

——. "The Politics of Poetics: Or, What Am I, a Critic, Doing in This Text?" In María Herrera-Sobek and Helena María Viramontes, eds., "Chicana Creativity and Criticism: Charting New Frontiers in American Literature." Special issue: *The Americas Review* 15 (1987): 3–4, 129–138.

——. *Women Singing in the Snow: A Cultural Analysis of Chicana Literature.* Tucson: University of Arizona Press, 1995.

——, and Eliana S. Rivero, eds. *Infinite Divisions: An Anthology of Chicana Literature.* Tucson: University of Arizona Press, 1993.

Rivera, Tomás. . . . *Y no se lo tragó la tierra/And the Earth Did Not Part.* Berkeley: Quinto Sol Publications, 1971.

Rodríguez, Jeanette. *Our Lady of Guadalupe.* Austin: University of Texas Press, 1994.

Rosaldo, Renato. *Culture and Truth: The Remaking of Social Analysis.* Boston: Beacon Press, 1989.

——. "Fables of the Fallen Guy." *Criticism in the Borderlands,* ed. Héctor Calderón and José Saldívar, 84–93. Durham. N.C.: Duke University Press, 1991.

Ruiz, Vicki L. "'And Miles to Go . . .': Mexican Women and Work, 1930–1985." In *Western Women: Their Lands, Their Lives,* ed. Lillian Schlissel, Vicki L. Ruiz, and Janice Monk, 117–136. Albuquerque: University of New Mexico Press, 1988.

Said, Edward W. "Traveling Theory." In *The World, the Text, and the Critic,* 226–247. Cambridge, Mass.: Harvard University Press, 1983.

Saldívar, José. *The Dialectics of Our America: Genealogy, Cultural Critique, and Literary History.* Durham, N.C.: Duke University Press, 1991.

Saldívar, José, and Héctor Calderón, eds. *Criticism in The Borderlands: Studies in Chicano Literature, Culture and Ideology.* Durham, N.C.: Duke University Press, 1991.

Saldívar, Ramón. *Chicano Narrative: The Dialectics of Difference.* Madison: University of Wisconsin Press, 1990.

Saldívar-Hull, Sonia. "Feminism on the Border: From Gender Politics to Geopolitics." In *Criticism in the Borderlands: Studies in Chicano Literature, Culture, and Ideology,* ed. José Saldívar and Héctor Calderón, 203–220. Durham, N.C.: Duke University Press, 1991.

———. "Mujeres en lucha/Mujeres de Fuerza: Women in Struggle/Women of Strength in Sandra Cisneros' Border Narratives." In *Feminism on the Border: Chicana Gender Politics and Literature,* 81–124. Berkeley & Los Angeles: University of California Press.

Salinas, Judy. "The Image of Woman in Chicano Literature." *Revista Chicano-Riqueña* 4, no. 4 (Fall 1976): 139–148.

Sánchez, Marta Ester. *Contemporary Chicana Poetry: A Critical Approach to an Emerging Literature.* Berkeley & Los Angeles: University of California Press, 1985.

Sánchez, Rita. "Chicana Writer Breaking Out of Silence." *De Colores* 3, no. 3 (1977): 31–37.

Sánchez, Rosaura. "Postmodernism and Chicano Literature." *Aztlán* 18, no. 2 (1987): 1–14.

———, and Rosa Martínez-Cruz. *Essays on la Mujer.* Los Angeles: Chicano Studies Center Publications, University of California, Los Angeles, 1977.

Sandoval, Chela. "U.S. Third World Feminism: The Theory and Method of Oppositional Consciousness in the Postmodern World." *Genders,* no. 10 (Spring 1991): 1–24.

Saporta-Sternbach, Nancy, et al. "Feminisms in Latin America: From Bogotá to San Bernardo." *Signs: Journal of Women in Culture & Society* 17, no. 2 (1992): 393–433.

Schmidt, Heide. "La risa: Etapas en la narrativa femenina en México y Alemania: Una aproximación." *Escritura: Revista de Teoría y Crítica Literarias* 16, nos. 31–32 (1991): 247–257.

Segovia, Miguel A. "Only Cauldrons Know the Secrets of Their Soups: Queer Romance and *Like Water for Chocolate.*" In *Velvet*

*Barrios: Popular Culture and Chicana/o Sexualities,* ed. Alicia Gaspar de Alba, 163–177. New York: Palgrave Macmillan.

Showalter, Elaine. *Women's Liberation and Literature.* New York, Harcourt Brace Jovanovich, 1971.

Soto, Shirlene A. *The Mexican Woman: A Study of Her Participation in the Revolution, 1910–1940.* Palo Alto, Calif.: R & E Publications, 1979.

———. "Tres modelos culturales: La Virgen de Guadalupe, la Malinche y la Llorona." *Fem* 10, no. 48 (1986): 13–16.

Steele, Cynthia. "The Other Within: Class and Ethnicity as Difference in Mexican Women's Literature." In *Cultural and Historical Grounding for Hispanic and Luso-Brazilian Feminist Literary Criticism,* ed. Hernán Vidal, 297–328. Minneapolis, Minn.: Institute for the Study of Ideologies and Literature, 1989.

Tabor, Mary B. W. "At the Library with Sandra Cisneros: A Solo Traveler in Two Worlds." *New York Times* (3 Jan. 1993), late ed.-final.

Trujillo, Carla, ed. *Living Chicana Theory.* Berkeley, CA: Third Woman Press, 1998.

———. *Chicana Lesbians: The Girls Our Mothers Warned Us About.* Berkeley, Calif.: Third Woman Press, 1991.

Tula, María Teresa. *Hear My Testimony: María Teresa Tula, Human Rights Activist of El Salvador.* Trans. and ed. Lynn Stephen. Boston: South End Press, 1994.

Tuñes, Pablo. *Mujeres en México: Una historia olvidada.* Mexico City: Planeta, 1987.

Urrutia, Elena, ed. *Imagen y realidad de la mujer.* Mexico City: SepSetentas, 1975.

Villanueva, Alma. "The Birthing of the Poetic 'I' in Alma Villanueva's Mother, May I? The Search for a Feminine Identity." In *Contemporary Chicana Poetry: A Critical Approach to an Emerging Literature,* Marta E. Sánchez, 24–84. Berkeley & Los Angeles: University of California Press, 1992.

———. *Mother, May I?* Pittsburgh: Motheroot Press, 1978.

Villarreal, José Antonio. *Pocho.* Garden City, N.Y.: Anchor Books, 1959.

Viramontes, Helena María. *The Moths and Other Stories.* Houston, Tex.: Arte Público Press, 1985.

———. "Nopalitos." In *Making Face, Making Soul=Haciendo Caras: Creative and Critical Perspectives by Women of Color,* ed.

Gloria Anzaldúa, 291–294. San Francisco: Aunt Lute Foundation Books, 1990.

———. "Tears on My Pillow." In *New Chicana/o Writing,* ed. Charles Tatum, vol. 1, 110–115. Tucson: University of Arizona Press, 1992.

———. *Under the Feet of Jesus.* New York: Dutton Press, 1995.

Walker, Alice. *In Search of Our Mothers' Gardens: Womanist Prose.* San Diego, Calif.: Harcourt Brace Jovanovic, 1983.

Winkler, Helga. "Selected Mexicana and Chicana Fiction: New Perspectives on History, Culture and Society." PhD diss., University of Texas at Austin, 1992.

Woolf, Virginia. *A Room of One's Own.* New York: Brace and World, 1929.

Yarbro-Bejarano, Yvonne. "Chicana Literature from a Chicana Feminist Perspective." *Feminisms: An Anthology of Literary Theory and Criticism,* ed. Robyn R. Warhol and Diane Price Herndl, 731–737. New Brunswick: Rutgers University Press, 1991.

Zeff, Jacqueline. "'What Doesn't Kill You, Makes You Fat': The Language of Food in Latina Literature." *Journal of American and Comparative Cultures* 25 (2002): 94–99.

Zimmerman, Marc. *U.S. Latino Literature: An Essay and Annotated Bibliography.* Chicago: MARCH/Abrazo Press, 1992.

# INDEX

"The Development of Chicana Feminist Discourse, 1970–1980" (Garcia), 10
"dialectics of difference," 3, 100n5
*The Dialectics of Our America*, (Saldívar-Hull), 4, 5
Diego, Juan, 14–15
*Diosa y Hembra* (Cotera), 10
*Do the Americas Have a Common Literature?* (Perez-Firmat), 4–5
*La doble jornada* (Mexico City), 9
domestic violence, 7, 9, 37, 38
Dutton Press, 68

El Salvador, 77, 107n9
Enriquez, Evangelina, 13
Esquivel, Laura, 18, 57, 60, 104n2; *Como agua para Chocolate* (*Like Water for Chocolate*), 17, 45, 58, 64
*Essays on la Mujer* (Martinez-Cruz), 10

family, 8, 17–18, 19, 102
father, 54–57
*Fem*, 9
feminism, 6, 58; border, 8, 20–21, 70; bridge, 19; Chicana/Mexicana, 9, 11, 100n13; Hispanic, 5; international, 17; Latin American, 5, 11; third-world, 18, 65, 102n3; transnational, 91, 93–94; U.S., 10
"Feminism on the Border" (Saldívar-Hull), 3
"Feminisms in Latin America" (Saporta-Sternbach), 10

*Feminist Theory from Margin to Center* (hooks), 107n4
Fernández Retamar, Roberto, 4
food: and healing, 62–63; importance in Chicana literature, 58–60
Franco, Jean, 38, 103n5; *Plotting Women*, 7, 11
Freire, Paulo, 90–91
Friedman, Tomas: *The Lexus and the Olive Tree*, 25

Galarza, Ernesto, 2
Gaona, Eugenia, 96
Garcia, Alma, "The Development of Chicana Feminist Discourse, 1970–1980," 10
garden, as site of female creativity, 46
Garden of Eden, 26–27
Garro, Elena, 104n2
gay/lesbian writing, 46
gender, 2, 17
*Giving Up the Ghost* (Moraga), 8
González, Deena: on La Malinche, 101n15, 102n1
González, Rodolpho, 2
grito, 43
El Grito de Dolores, 40, 103n16
La Gritona, 35–36, 37, 43, 47, 103n17
Gutiérrez-Jones, Carl, *Rethinking the Borderlands*, 3

Harlequin Romances, 103n16
*Hasta no verte Jesús mío* (Poniatowska), 8
healing, 61. *See also* food
hegemony, 20